Motivating People
for Improved Performance

The Results-Driven Manager Series

The Results-Driven Manager series collects timely articles from *Harvard Management Update* and *Harvard Management Communication Letter* to help senior to middle managers sharpen their skills, increase their effectiveness, and gain a competitive edge. Presented in a concise, accessible format to save managers valuable time, these books offer authoritative insights and techniques for improving job performance and achieving immediate results.

Other books in the series:

Teams That Click

Presentations That Persuade and Motivate

Face-to-Face Communications for Clarity and Impact

Winning Negotiations That Preserve Relationships

Managing Yourself for the Career You Want

Getting People on Board

Taking Control of Your Time

Dealing with Difficult People

Managing Change To Reduce Resistance

Becoming an Effective Leader

A Timesaving Guide

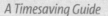

THE RESULTS-DRIVEN MANAGER

Motivating People for Improved Performance

• • •

Harvard Business School Press

Boston, Massachusetts

Library of Congress Cataloging-in-Publication Data

The results-driven manager : motivating people for improved
performance.
        p.   cm. — (The results-driven manager series)
     ISBN 1-59139-779-0
  1. Employee motivation. 2. Supervision of employees.
3. Performance—Management. I. Harvard Business School
Press. II. Series.
     HF5549.5.M63R47 2005
     658.3'14—dc22   2004021243

The paper used in this publication meets the requirements of the
American National Standard for Permanence of Paper for Publications
and Documents in Libraries and Archives Z39.48-1992.

Contents

Contents

Retaining Your Top Performers

Selecting the Right Rewards, Recognition, and Incentives

Contents

Introduction

• • •

You've got a talented group working for you—people with the skills and expertise your company needs to succeed. But all that talent is meaningless unless you motivate your people to produce their best results on the job. When employees feel inspired to live up to their full potential in the workplace, their companies excel. Imagine a team in which everyone performs at his or her highest level. You might see characteristics such as the following:

- People generate fresh solutions to the company's most pressing problems.

- Teams collaborate to create innovative products and services that revolutionize the marketplace.

- Employees enthusiastically give their energy, time, and dedication to the company.

- People remain loyal to the organization even during tough times.

- Everyone feels stimulated by the challenges of his or her role.

- Employees take pride in their work and feel accountable for the company's future.

A workforce with these sterling qualities can vault a company far ahead of its rivals.

Motivation: More Important Than Ever

In light of today's business conditions, motivating people to be their best has become more crucial than ever. Why? Profit margins have thinned and, for some companies, virtually disappeared in the face of ever-stiffening competition. Economic uncertainty has crippled entire industries—and no one can predict with any accuracy when hard times will give way to better times. Only through motivation can managers help their employees generate the excellent performance that enables companies to boost profitability and survive—even thrive— during tough times.

But even a healthy economy is no guarantee that a company will get the most from its employees. That's because, with economic success, many people no longer feel satisfied with a job that merely pays the bills. They want *meaningful* work. That is, they want to feel part of something larger than themselves, to be challenged, to sharpen their skills, and to give their dedication to an organization that they believe is doing great things. For many employees today, a steady paycheck alone won't motivate them to excel.

Moreover, businesses have become embroiled in a war for talent that shows no signs of abating. In fact, owing to demographic changes, the battle for valued employees in the United States alone is expected to continue to rage for the next several decades. That's because the principal talent pool—workers under age forty-five—will shrink by 6 percent over the next ten years as birthrates decline and the population ages. Given these conditions, it's not surprising that job mobility remains brisk, as people seek work that offers them meaning, satisfaction, and a sense of challenge in addition to financial reward.

Clearly, managers must make motivating employees an integral part of the job if they hope to build the kind of workforce their company needs to succeed—and if they want to advance and excel in their own careers. But motivating others to be their best can be surprisingly difficult.

A Complex Art

For many people, the word *motivate* has connotations of physical movement—*impel* is one synonym for it. Yet managers seeking to motivate their employees can't simply push them, physically or through instilling fear, to perform. True motivation is far more complex than that and requires an artful blend of managerial skills.

To inspire your people to excel, you need to help them find meaning in their work and feel productive on the job. You also have to encourage the personal qualities that enhance employees' performance—such as the ability to view the world with both optimism and realism, to feel the same dedication to the company that an owner feels, and to trust in the organization's capacity to succeed.

You must also foster commitment *beyond* the immediate job in question. In a motivated team, people energize one another toward better performance. They take responsibility for whole business processes, not just their own tasks. And they work to transfer successful practices across the entire organization. They understand how their efforts impact the company's bottom line and feel accountable for overall financial performance.

But once you've achieved all this, you can't stop there. You've got to identify your *best* performers—those whom you believe the company needs to survive—and devise ways to win their loyalty. The right system of rewards, recognition, and incentives, among other things, will determine whether your talent-management plan succeeds or fails.

The articles in this collection are organized into sections that address each of these themes. Here's a preview of what you'll find in each section:

Helping Employees Find Meaning

To find meaning in their work, people at every organizational level—from the front lines all the way to the corner-office suite—must believe that their efforts matter and must have continual opportunities to learn. With that in mind, Charles Wardell opens this section with "Building Front-Line Morale." Managers, Wardell explains, don't need expensive training programs or benefit and compensation plans to help front-line employees be productive and feel enthusiastic about their work. Instead, he points out, "you can make a big difference . . . simply by the way you run your shop." Wardell offers five quick tips, including *viewing employees as customers* (greeting them when they arrive, saying good-bye when they leave, and talking with them in between), *listening* (asking people what skills they want to develop), and *cross-training* to provide constant on-the-job learning.

In "Enlisting Hearts and Minds," Loren Gary describes ways to help employees see how the company's work and their own search for meaning are connected. He reminds managers that fear and coercion don't cultivate a sense of meaning—especially in an age when "companies are asking for increasingly higher levels of commitment from their employees in return for the hollow assurance that they'll have improved their skill sets by the time they're outsourced." Instead, managers must demonstrate their commitment to loyalty and trust by "letting employees know what you know" about the company's financial situation and business plans. This fosters a sense of mutual partnership, and the highly motivating sense that "we're all in this together."

Adam Tobler explores this section's theme further in "Making Work Meaningful." In his view, managers need to understand the values to which each employee responds and design work that taps into those "intrinsic rewards." Tobler cites expert Michael Maccoby's model of five "character types": *experts* are motivated by mastery; *helpers,* by caring for people; *defenders,* by protecting their self-esteem and survival. *Innovators* respond to creating and experimenting; and *self-developers,* to balancing competence with personal growth.

In "Speak to What Drives Them," Anne Field offers a different intrinsic-reward model based on eight "career anchors." These anchors include technical/functional competence, managerial competence, autonomy, security, entrepreneurial creativity, a sense of service, pure challenge, and ability to balance work life with private life. To motivate people, managers must tailor their communication style and recognition systems to each employee based on his or her anchor. For example, with employees motivated by technical competence, "don't try to fake [your knowledge]. They'll see through you immediately and lose respect for you." Recognize such employees by enabling them to constantly hone their craft and stay current with the latest developments.

Loren Gary concludes this section with "The Search for Meaningful Work." He takes a closer look at entrepreneurial spirit, maintaining that "free agency" (employees' capitalizing on their own "intellectual property") is becoming more possible for a greater number of people, thanks to expanding economies. To benefit from entrepreneurial energy, passion, and creativity, even growing companies "must preserve an intimate, entrepreneurial environment" that makes free agents "want to affiliate with them. It's only by attracting such experienced talent that companies can hope to be competitive."

Strengthening Personal Qualities

People who are motivated and who perform at their best not only view their work as meaningful, they also demonstrate specific personal qualities that managers can help develop. In "Staying Positive—Without the Illusions," Loren Gary explores one of these traits: *resilience*. A blend of optimism and realism, resilience enables employees to "add accuracy and flexibility to [their] habitual way of thinking about problems." Gary maintains that managers can help build employees' resilience by strengthening the optimism or realism half of the equation as needed. For example, one manager helped an employee balance an overly liberal supply of optimism with greater perspective on potentially adverse situations.

The employee listed possible negative implications of a situation he was facing, and assigned a likelihood to each. Then he fleshed out the *most* likely outcomes and developed solutions for them.

In addition to resilience, highly motivated employees take *pride* in their work—a trait that Theodore Kinni examines in "Working Like an Owner." "To make a commitment to communicating about pride," Kinni writes, "is to tap into a very powerful motivating force." Kinni advises managers to reinforce employees' pride by recognizing the value of their work for the company's bottom line and by explaining why certain kinds of performance (such as accurate measurement or skilled use of a piece of equipment) are vital to the organization's survival. Even if the company's current financial performance doesn't evoke pride, there are many other sources—such as pride in one's colleagues, in the company's heritage, and in the products or services that the organization offers customers.

Trust—between managers and employees—constitutes another ingredient of motivation, as explained in the article "Trust: How to Build It, Earn It—and Reestablish It When It's Broken." Trust enables people in organizations to work together more effectively. To wring tangible results from this quality, managers must behave in ways that promote three kinds of trust. For example, to build *competence trust,* acknowledge employees' skills and abilities and let them make decisions. To build *contractual trust,* delegate appropriately, keep agreements, and be consistent. And to build communication trust, share information, tell the truth, and admit mistakes. Also "develop your own capacity for trust . . . When you believe that you are dependable and reliable, you have confidence when dealing with the unknown. Your ability to trust others grows with your own ability to trust yourself."

"The Rise of Hyperarchies," by Loren Gary, examines trust from another angle. According to Gary, employees who believe that their manager sees them as trusted contributors feel highly motivated to perform. Trust becomes especially powerful in a *hyperarchy,* defined in Gary's article as "a large-scale, self-organizing community that [unleashes] unusually high degrees of energy and engagement—despite the lack of clear or direct economic payoff for participants." Examples of hyperarchies include Linux (the open-source software movement) and Toyota's famously lean supply chain. Hyperarchic organizations thrive on trust, because "they allow participants to largely choose their own tasks, operate at their own pace, and derive satisfaction from the work itself."

In "High-Performance Prison," the section's final article, Jennifer McFarland defines a not-so-desirable personal trait characterizing highly motivated employees: "gonzo overindulgence." Defined as "the addictive, almost erotic, appeal that deep and obsessive involvement in a task can have," gonzo overindulgence can lead to burnout if employees don't take preventive steps. Managers must help their people by avoiding the common—and understandable—tendency to overload star performers who will "work themselves to death to get it done."

Fostering Commitment
Beyond Just the Job

Motivated employees care about more than just their own jobs or the task currently at hand. They commit to enhancing performance across their entire organization. In "How to Energize Colleagues with Wayne Baker," Baker, a professor at the University of Michigan Business School, discusses the importance of employees energizing others in their organizational networks. Energizers, Baker explains, focus on possibilities rather than problems, help others feel fully engaged, learn from colleagues, and speak their mind. The more energized people feel, the higher their performance. By modeling energizing attitudes and behaviors, managers can motivate their own employees to excel—and encourage them, in turn, to energize others.

In addition to inspiring others in their organizational networks, motivated workers take responsibility for the quality of entire business processes, not just the parts of a process that they happen to work in. John Case turns to this subject in "What You Can Learn from Open-Book Management." According to Case, people feel more motivated to improve a process when they know what's going on—that is, they understand the business's fundamental objectives and ways of measuring progress toward those goals. Companies can strengthen this understanding by sharing financial information with employees, explaining the information's context, and discussing how smaller departmental objectives support larger corporate-level strategic efforts. Of course, Case notes, "there is always key data that companies must protect. But open-book companies find they can share much more information with employees than they once thought safe . . . [Such companies] are dedicated to the idea that employees can't work effectively in the dark."

In "Debriefing Gabriel Szulanski: Improving Best-Practice Transfer," INSEAD professor Szulanski, interviewed by Lauren Keller Johnson, stresses the importance of spreading effective practices across organizations. Transfer of best practices occurs more frequently—and is more successful—when employees feel motivated to take responsibility for their company's overall performance. To inspire best-practice transfer, managers can take steps to "unstick" knowledge. These steps include encouraging people to use transferred knowledge enough to embed it in the way they do their work, challenging employees to identify opportunities to leverage existing knowledge, and cultivating a history of positive communication and collaboration among their teams. Additional techniques include explaining the value of new knowledge and ensuring that people have the skills, shared language, and experience to put that knowledge to work.

In addition to feeling accountable to peers, processes, and best-practice transfer, motivated employees have the same sense of ownership of their company that true owners possess. They feel responsible for the company's very survival and future. The final article in this section is a question and answer session with Jack Stack, CEO of Springfield Remanufacturing Corporation. In "Are Your Employees Invested in the Bottom Line?" Stack explains how managers can cultivate this sense of ownership among employees. His suggestions include the following: help employees look holistically at the business—at how "all the parts, such as R&D, marketing, customer service, and finance, fit together"; foster business literacy—understanding of basic financial information; and explain how employees' actions directly influence financial performance. For example, one company told employees that reducing accounts receivable turnover drives down debt, which yields higher net income. Money saved on interest expense also boosts profits. To motivate people to reduce accounts receivable turnover, the company put a portion of the improved cash flow in a special employees' bonus program—making it very obvious to people how they could make a difference.

Retaining Your Top Performers

Don't assume that you need to focus your motivational abilities on employees who are struggling or who somehow aren't living up to their potential. Your ability to motivate is equally—if not more—crucial when it comes to your star performers. Since you're already getting top-quality work from these talented individuals, you want to concentrate your motivational efforts on another goal: securing their loyalty to the company.

The articles in this section describe powerful techniques for retaining your best employees. In "Time to Get Serious About Talent Management," Kristen B. Donahue offers four recommendations: 1) aim for retention of top people and attrition of low performers; 2) enhance collaboration and cooperation among talented direct reports: "[People] are loyal to their groups. So make the groups stronger"; 3) identify people "for whom loyalty, community building, and being part of something bigger than themselves matter a great deal"—and invest your efforts in retaining them; and 4) match star performers to work that challenges them to develop their skills—and give them adequate resources and some control over their own work.

"A New Retention Strategy: Focusing on Individuals" augments Donahue's ideas with additional suggestions. For example, consider instituting "stay interviews"—conversations with valued employees about how they're enjoying their jobs, what they'd like to do next, and so on. Experts recommend conducting such interviews regularly and keeping an ear out for early signs of discontent, such as unexplained absences. Your goal? To talk with people *before* they leave, not just *when* they leave. In addition to using stay interviews, hire for retention. Bring in employees who fit with your company's values, whether it's stability and predictability or an ability to deal with ambiguity and uncertainty. Don't soft-pedal less appealing elements of an open position—you want people who want the job "warts and all."

Good people stay on board longer when they like and respect their supervisor, as revealed in "Nine Steps Toward Creating a Great Workplace." According to one Gallup senior vice president, "people may join a company because of its brand identity, but how long they stay depends . . . on the quality of their manager." To secure valued employees' loyalty, consider these ideas: Help them see the purpose and importance of what they do—even seemingly minor tasks such as writing reports. Expect the most from people, and challenge them to exceed their goals. Set high standards, but don't dictate how your employees meet them. And spend at least 10 percent of your time talking with employees about their agendas.

The section concludes with Frederick F. Reichheld's "Satisfaction: The False Path to Employee Loyalty." In this provocative article, Reichheld challenges the often-advanced claim that loyal employees are satisfied ones.

Instead, "real employee loyalty is generated when employees, unhappy with the status quo, are constantly reaching to deliver the kind of value and service that develops increasingly loyal customers." To strengthen the link between employee and customer loyalty, Reichheld advises managers to structure their departments or units into small teams of eight to twelve members. Teams in this size range are more responsive to customers' needs and feel a stronger sense of accountability than larger teams do. Reichheld adds: "Provide your teams with the tools they need to monitor how well they're creating the kind of value necessary to earn customer loyalty."

Selecting the Right Rewards, Recognition, and Incentives

Too many managers assume that a salary increase, bonus, or some other monetary reward is enough to motivate employees to excel. As the articles in this section demonstrate, money certainly constitutes an important reward in the workplace. But the most motivating rewards, recognition, and incentives comprise a *mix* of monetary and nonmonetary forms. Indeed, some experts argue that nonmonetary rewards can have a far more motivating influence than monetary forms.

For example, in "Employee Recognition and Reward with Bob Nelson," Nelson stresses the importance of informal recognition in stepping up employee motivation. According to Nelson, employees *most* value managerial support and involvement—being asked their opinions, participating in decisions, having authority to do their jobs, and getting support when they've made a mistake. They also value basic praise—whether it's delivered face to face, in writing, in public, or by e-mail. "Those are the hottest [motivations] for people," Nelson points out, "and none of them costs a dime."

Loren Gary examines the notion of monetary rewards from a different perspective in "Rethinking Money and Motivation." During flush economic times, Gary writes, people assume that their income will always go up, and many begin to see the accumulation of money as the most tangible indicator that they're doing work that matters. The problem is that, if the economy flags and the company doesn't give an annual pay increase, employees conclude that it doesn't respect or value them— a surefire way to dampen motivation. To dispel this notion, managers must educate employees on basic business finance—explaining the difference between the company's revenues and its profitability, and showing them how their work contributes to the bottom line. The ultimate goal? To help employees identify *true* sources of on-the-job fulfillment that money can never provide.

In "Which Incentives Pay Off Now?" Peter Jacobs describes innovations in long-term incentive plans. In particular, Jacobs relates how many companies are reconsidering the role of stock options in employee remuneration—and blazing new trails in the realm of variable compensation. With variable compensation, employees can select from a menu that might include cash, restricted shares, and options. The variable portion of compensation gets paid only when the company achieves performance targets. When people have a direct line of sight between their on-the-job performance and the rewards they receive, motivation intensifies.

Clearly, motivating people to be their best requires complex approaches and a deep understanding of human nature. As you read the articles in this collection, ask yourself:

- Do your employees find meaning and purpose in their work? If not, what might you do to help them find it?

- Do your employees demonstrate the personal qualities that enhance performance, such as blending optimism with realism, viewing themselves as owners of the business, trusting you and the company, and knowing how to avoid burnout? If not, how can you help them develop these qualities?

- Do your employees commit themselves to more than just their own jobs—for example, do they energize peers, take responsibility for whole business processes, transfer best practices across departments and functions, and feel directly accountable for the company's bottom line? If not, how can you foster this broader commitment?

- Do you know who your top performers are? If so, what are you doing to retain them?

- What rewards, recognition, and incentives do you use to motivate your people? How might you fine-tune these to better motivate employees?

By using the ideas in this volume to motivate your people to be their best, you'll generate impressive results for your company and achieve success in your career as well.

Helping
Employees
Find Meaning

• • •

The most motivated employees feel that their work matters—that they're contributing to something larger than themselves. But how do you help your people find this sense of meaning in their work? As you'll discover in this section's articles, you don't need expensive training programs or complex compensation plans. Instead, create a sense of "we're all in this together" by sharing what you know about the company's business plans. Get to know what motivates each of your employees—whether it's mastery of a particular technology, opportunities to create something new, or the chance to express their entrepreneurial spirit. Then adapt your communication style and recognition systems to each of these "intrinsic rewards."

Building Front-Line Morale

• • •

Charles Wardell

They're the people who make any business go: store clerks, warehouse workers, housekeepers, telephone reps, and all the other front-line employees who do companies' everyday work. They rarely have much training and don't make big salaries. Yet they're often the very people who determine whether a customer goes away satisfied or annoyed. How can you help them be productive and feel enthusiastic about their work?

There are two expensive approaches. One is to develop a comprehensive training program, helping front-line people acquire the skills they need to succeed in their work and advance in an organization. The other is to provide better benefits and compensation than front-line workers usually get. (Think of Starbucks's stock options.) Both can work wonders. But if you're responsible for front-line employees and you're not in a position to implement such programs, don't despair—there's a third approach, and it's cheap. You yourself can make a big difference to front-line employees simply by the way you run your shop.

Check Your Attitude

Do Dilbert cartoons turn up regularly on your wall? "A lot of managers have a hard time trusting front-line people," says Bob Nelson of Nelson Motivation. "They say that the pay is lousy, that it's hard to find good people, that no one would take these jobs who didn't have to, and that employees don't stick around long enough to make it worthwhile to train them." Not surprisingly, these managers treat front-line people like used furniture. "You don't understand," one manager told Nelson. "My people are *defective*."

Compare this attitude with that of Joe Clark, operator of a Chick-fil-A restaurant. "The people who work for me are my customers," says Clark. He greets them when they arrive, says goodbye when they leave, and talks with them in between. "The most fun I have is right before we open, when everyone is doing food prep," he says. "It's an opportunity for us to catch up with each other."

Clark is in the fast-food business, but some of his employees have been with him for eight, nine, even ten years. "They've found job satisfaction right here."

Do the Easy Things First—and Often

Kathe Farris is a recognition consultant with Fleet Boston, and a few years ago asked a group of proof encoders—people who process checks—to list the top three things managers could do to make them want to keep working for the bank. Their answers? "Say hello, say thank you, and say please," she says. That answer jibes with research done a few years ago by Gerald Graham, dean of Barton School of Business at Wichita State University. Graham surveyed office workers and health-care employees to find out what incentives had the greatest effect on productivity. "The interesting thing," he reports, "was that the zero-cost items were the ones employees said have the most impact." These included personal notes, public recognition, and morale-building meetings to celebrate successes. "Not many of us do these things well."

Listen, Then Act

Good managers, says Nelson, check in with their employees regularly. One goal: getting to know one another. Ask people why they came to work for you rather than someone else, and what they like and dislike about the job. Find out what their hobbies are and what skills they want to develop. If you manage a store, you may find that one of your employees loves organizing displays; asking her to do so will build enthusiasm. Another goal: learning what employees know. "Never underestimate the knowledge and skills of the people you've been charged to lead," advises Steve Bauman, Marriott International's VP for management staffing and development. "These are the people who know what it takes to do a job. When a housekeeping supervisor has an opinion on how to best organize her staff, you might want to step back and listen."

A willingness to listen can turn an entire unit around. Sharon Decker was VP in charge of customer service at Duke Power, where she supervised the utility's call center. Michael Landrum, the company's HR manager, remembers that Decker's people would do anything for her. Her secret, says Decker, was that she formed task groups around employee recognition and rewarded employees the way they wanted to be rewarded. "It was a stressful job," she recalls, and what the employees wanted were opportunities to relieve the stress. "Doing fun things—covered-dish lunches, extra breaks, funny skits on employee recognition day—really livened up the workplace."

Listening can also turn up ideas you'd never come up with on your own. One company, Nelson reports, employs a lot of college students. The manager learned that they needed a quiet place to study, so the company set up a study area in a spare office. The students felt listened to and valued, hence positive toward the company. "When they're not working they come in and study. When the company is in a crunch, they're willing to jump in and help."

Cross Train

Does it need to be said? Most people are more motivated when they're learning something than when they're not. Chick-fil-A's Clark, for example, tries to expose all his employees to all the jobs in his store. "One day an employee might work the cash register, while the next day he might be making sandwiches." Not only does this make the job more interesting for the employees, it also makes them better able to help one another when the need arises.

Set an Example

An article in the May–June 1999 *Harvard Business Review* describes how the U.S. Marine Corps—which hires a lot of young, unskilled, and sometimes troubled youth—manages to "outperform all other organizations when it comes to engaging the hearts and minds of the front line." One key: leadership by example. "Our highest priority was the lowest-ranking individual rifleman," recalls coauthor Jason Santamaria, a former USMC officer who is now a business analyst with McKinsey & Co. "For instance, Marine officers never eat until their Marines have." Santamaria estimates he spent between 50% and 90% of his time working directly with the people who reported to him.

Leading by example includes being willing to roll up your sleeves. Southwest Airlines CEO Herb Kelleher is famous for the days he spends working the gates and handling baggage. Bauman's first exposure to Marriott was in 1987, when he was sent there as an army officer to observe management behavior. "The manager of this hotel was impeccably dressed," he recalls, "but if he saw a piece of trash on the ground, he would pick it up and put it in his pocket."

Marriott, like the Marine Corps, has a well-defined set of values. But what if your company's values aren't as clear? "You have to articulate them yourself," says Bauman. But, he adds, that's the easy part. "The hard part is constant reinforcement of those values. You need to recognize people when they do something that exemplifies the values that you want them to aspire to."

Reprint U9905C

Enlisting Hearts and Minds

. . .

Loren Gary

The old understanding that an organization would guarantee you a job for life has been dead for some time, but we still see companies asking for increasingly higher levels of commitment from their employees in return for the hollow assurance that they'll have improved their skill sets by the time they're outsourced. The reaction of many workers is to retreat within the narrow confines of what they can control on the job.

This type of response is sad enough from an individual perspective, but organizationally it can be downright crippling. John Kotter, former Matsushita Professor of Leadership at Harvard Business School, has observed that only those companies whose employees are "intellectually and emotionally convinced that their business creates something that adds value to the world" will survive in the new economy. But in an economic climate characterized by rapid change and job anxiety, can companies legitimately expect their employees to bring their hearts and minds to the workplace? And if so, what do employers need to be willing to do to make this happen?

Fear and Coercion Don't Work

"As your manager, I can't touch your heart and soul by threatening you—they are gifts that you choose to give," says Richard N. Knowles, a plant manager at DuPont for 13 years. "My job as a manager is to create the conditions that make you want to give those gifts, that make you want to develop as a whole person instead of just as a 'worker.'"

"It is impossible to get people to put their hearts and souls into the workplace through fear," confirms Kotter. "Fear leads to compliance behavior, which eventually leads to hate." And yet, there are more than a few corporate heads claiming dramatic results from scare tactics; turnaround king Al Dunlap is the most celebrated current example. "There is only a narrow set of circumstances in which such an approach can work," Kotter cautions. "If the threatening approach is able in a relatively short time frame to produce benefits that are shared widely enough so that employees' behavior changes, the Dunlaps can put their guns away. But fear tends to turn off workers' creativity, and in this day and age it's hard to find many circumstances in which companies don't need their employees' creativity."

Compensation Alone
Is Not the Answer

People need to be paid equitably for the work they do, but this doesn't mean that you have to pay the highest salaries in your field to get exemplary commitment. "Understanding the basis for the compensation package is more important," says Laura Avakian, senior vice president for human resources at the Beth Israel-Deaconess hospitals in Boston. "It's a matter of giving people information about how compensation decisions are made— and giving them the freedom to question it."

Never Underestimate the
Power of Sharing Information

There's no quicker way to demonstrate your commitment to loyalty and trust than to let employees know what you know. "There's nothing magical about it," Avakian claims, "but as much as possible we try to make sure that employees know as much as management does about our financial situation and our business plans." This, in turn, fosters a sense of "mutual partnership, an understanding that we're all in this together."

Avakian's former employer, Beth Israel Hospital, had a policy of never eliminating positions through layoffs—a remarkable commitment that it managed to live up to throughout its entire history, up to and including its 1996 merger with Deaconess Hospital. But this policy was sorely tested, as the hospital faced a potential deficit of $20 million. Management shared this baleful news with staff and asked for their help. Within ten days, it had received 4,000 cost-saving ideas from employees; 16 task forces were formed to deal with them. Most of the cost-saving strategies involved tighter controls on purchasing, but some of the most difficult suggestions—not taking raises and holding back the accrual of paid time off—were suggested by staff. By the end of the year, sufficient savings had been realized to avert any layoffs.

Focusing on Values Beyond Profitability May Be the Best Way to Ensure Profitability

"We still haven't learned that you can't enroll people's loyalty and creativity if you're not willing to enlarge the purpose of the work in ways far beyond money making," observes Margaret Wheatley, a renowned expert on new modes of organization. "Compared to management, employees tend to have a much greater systems or global consciousness about their work. They want their work to connect to a greater purpose. Companies seem to have forgotten this in recent years, but people want to work in order to bring more good into the world. And the great irony in all this is that companies could be much more profitable if they took this into account."

The specifics of motivating different groups of employees will vary. For example, "Some clerical workers may not see themselves in the workplace forever," Kotter points out. "But they are still human beings, and by helping them understand how the work of the business and their own search for meaning are connected, you can elicit a level of interest and commitment that is rare."

Reprint U9702D

Making Work Meaningful

* * *

Adam Tobler

"Is that all there is?"

Some of us recognize this as the refrain from an old Peggy Lee song. And some of us know it as an inner tug, felt when a business trip returns us home too late to see the kids, or the latest skirmish in the battle for scarce resources at the office leaves us convinced that we're all missing the larger point. We work long, and hard, but the supports that previous generations might have counted on don't seem to be there for us.

A generation ago, a manager might have found relief from the dissatisfactions of an ill-suited job or the strictures of life as an Organization Man by compartmentalizing his life. The material rewards of work fell into one compartment; the rewards of family and community service into another. In yet another compartment, we had free time for activities that provided enjoyment and meaning. Now we don't. So we seek meaning from the life we have, most of which is invested in work.

To those of another generation, the idea of seeking meaning from work is a ridiculous one. But post–World War II managers and professionals have had increasingly little choice. According to the U.S. Census conducted in 1990, 87 percent of all married women in the American work force and 65 percent of all men are in two-job couples. But, in contrast to the labor-saving promises of the industrial age, all this work isn't buying us more leisure time. As Arlie Russell Hochschild, the author of *The Time Bind: When Work Becomes Home and Home Becomes Work,* has noted, the average American worker has 12 annual vacation days, compared to 30 in Germany, and 27 in Sweden. This means that, more and more, our "community" is where we work. And the old idea that we can stroll through life as compartmentalized beings, with material needs addressed on one side of some inner partition and human needs on another side, has become outdated. So the search has been on for solutions that allow us to be human, productive, and successful all at the same time.

Tall order, as a growing body of work/life literature suggests. The trick, those who would counsel us say, is to match ourselves to the "right" work, the right work environment, and to understand fully the role we want work to play in our lives.

Some entrepreneurs (and some book publishers) tell us that one way to find meaning in work is to ditch the big-company grind and go to work for the "new age" companies that advertise themselves as human-friendly, environmentally conscious, and otherwise enlightened. These are also the companies that market their products by advertising their company cultures. Among them are Tom's of Maine, the maker of natural toothpaste; The Body Shop, which retails cosmetics and beauty aids made in part from third-world ingredients; Ben & Jerry's, which makes high-fat ice creams named after counterculture heroes such as Jerry Garcia; and Starbucks, which has offered generous benefits packages to part-time workers, and seems to be selling coffee on every corner of America.

Along with offering high-end products to affluent baby boomers, many of these companies do indeed offer workplace environments that seek to make work more meaningful. Tom Chappell, the founder and head of Tom's of Maine, invites great theologians to company retreats and initiates company projects that benefit the rain forests. But jumping the large corporate ship in which you row to market upscale ice cream from the woods of Vermont isn't a plausible answer to everyman's, or everywoman's, search for meaning. And for many of us who wish to have more influence in the larger world, doing so would be unsatisfying.

In fact, some of the best places to work, historically, have been large companies—often companies that have strong core values that go well beyond financial ones. In *Built To Last: Successful Habits of Visionary Companies,* Jerry Porras and James C. Collins have chronicled 18 companies that turned in outstanding financial performances over the last 50 years. They concluded that Walt Disney, Hewlett-Packard, 3M, and other companies were able to manage such results because they enforced strong core values that allowed them to successfully undergo dramatic change through multiple product lifecycles and management changes. Paradoxically, these core principles did not arise from the pursuit of competitive advantage, but from other, more compelling values, such as respect for the individual (Hewlett- Packard) or innovation (3M). Porras and Collins suggest that these values, which are also the key ingredients to long-term performance, offer employees a more compelling mission at the office than mere pursuit of the bottom line.

For those of us who have contemplated chucking it all for a better berth, it is worth noting that none of the companies studied by Porras and Collins went out of their way to advertise their core values or mission statements in order to sell products or attract employees. The successful companies they examined simply went about their business with, for example, the management-by-walking-around of Bill Hewlett and David Packard. Such practices resulted in tremendous work force loyalty. This can be seen as a more meaningful workplace environment, since employees clearly wanted to be part of it.

The leadership of any company determines to a large extent how much employees can grow, develop, and find satisfaction in their work. Many of today's best leaders do not focus solely on financial results: They also think about the experiences and opportunities that provide employees with a sense of intrinsic reward at having built something substantial. At a conference Henry Schacht, the chairman of Lucent Technologies and former CEO of Cummins Engine, was asked about the kind of corporate culture he sought to build. He said that he strived for one where people could flourish and described the systematic way he has sought to build a culture in which people can do just that. While leading Cummins, Schacht not only allowed but encouraged managers to build competence in different functional areas before assuming general management responsibility. So a senior manager might have risen through personnel, then operations, then finance. Such experience builds a manager's cross-functional expertise and minimizes functional or departmental parochialism.

Make Your Own Work More Meaningful

Since the evidence suggests that it's not the size of the company, or the way it markets its products, itself, or its values that will guarantee you satisfaction at work, it's more useful to focus on where you work now and how your experience at work might be enriched. As a book about meditation titled *Wherever You Go, There You Are* suggests, changing location may not make all the difference in your life. Instead, doing what you can do right where you are might be the best first step to help you find meaning in work.

Your own compass determines what makes work meaningful to you. Different personality types find satisfaction in different ways.

What Makes You Work?

Yes, of course: the mortgage. But beyond basic material needs, what's the motivation that has driven you to the company, the job, the occupation, and the hours that occupy you now? Money is only part of what motivates us at work. People perform based on their ability and their motivation, and both defy simple explanation or predictability. Aside from financial and other external rewards, people act according to intrinsic rewards, according to Steven Kerr, author of *Ultimate Rewards: What Really Motivates People to Achieve*. The nature of these rewards varies by personality type.

Defining your personality type will help you understand the values that motivate you. In *Why Work? Motivating the New Work Force*, Michael Maccoby suggests that there are five different character types at work. Each responds to different values. Recognizing the kind of person you are will help determine what intrinsically motivates you. Here is Maccoby's list of character types:

- EXPERT: Motivated by mastery, control, autonomy. Example: Craftsman—Excellence in making things.

- HELPER: Motivated by relatedness, caring for people. Example: Company man—Helping authorities. Example: Institutional helper—Resolving conflict.

- DEFENDER: Motivated by protection, dignity. Example: Jungle fighter—Power, self-esteem, survival.

- INNOVATOR: Motivated by creating, experimenting. Example: Gamesman—Glory, competition.

- SELF-DEVELOPER: Motivated by balancing competence, play, knowledge, and personal growth.

A decade ago, Maccoby wrote that the "gamesman" represented the dominant business type—someone who valued short-term competition, transactions, and the "quick hit." Today's manager, says Maccoby, is the "self-developer"—a well-rounded person who seeks to balance personal growth, knowledge, and competence.

If you are an innovator, you will find your work most rewarding if you can spend much of your time creating and experimenting. You will find little meaning from work that stresses protection. The work that the expert will find most rewarding will emphasize mastery and control. She will find little reward in work that stresses harmonizing relationships.

Can Work Be a Calling?

Self-analysis, of course, has its limits, as does analysis by category. You are a category of one. And there is a larger plane upon which it may be helpful for you to fix yourself: your professional mission. Some people feel they have a mission in their work, and many of our most effective and respected leaders are among them. Others use the old-fashioned religious term "calling." It implies that what you have to contribute at work is unique, exceptional, and vital—a framework for viewing our place at work that may be especially useful for today's knowledge workers.

In the bestseller *The Soul's Code: In Search of Character and Calling*, theologian James Hillman says that each of us possesses a unique program for a unique life. If that sounds new age, uncomfortably religious, fatalistic, or otherwise unlikely, consider the extent to which pre-programming occurs in nature. Hillman uses the analogy of an acorn, which contains all the "coding" for the final tree—if only it is given enough water, soil, and sunlight. When adults, like errant acorns, find themselves "planted" in the wrong soil, with too little light or too much water, Hillman says, they should give up for a time on the idea of "growing up" like an acorn stretching to become an oak. Instead, he says, we must by self-examination "grow down" to rediscover our lost mission in life.

Here we come to one of the freshest and most critical of the new ideas about how we can find more meaning at work. The idea, postulated by Michael Novak, and many other business leaders, is that business itself can be a calling, and an honorable one. In *Business as a Calling: Work and the Examined Life,* Novak echoes Hillman and others by suggesting that a "calling" or mission is a path that brings intrinsic reward.

Novak's life illustrates his point, as well as the fact that many of us may not find our "mission" in the places that might seem most obvious. Novak studied for the priesthood for twelve and a half years, but abandoned his work five months before his scheduled ordination. He came to believe that it was not his "call." Mentors, colleagues, family, and friends thought he had lost his senses. But he felt strongly drawn to become a writer. Novak has since had a prolific career as a writer, speaker, ambassador, and winner of the Templeton Prize for Progress in Religion. In this last achievement he joins the company of Alexander Solzhenitsyn and Mother Theresa.

Andrew Carnegie, the poor son of a Scottish loom operator, discovered other types of missions—the first involving business, the next focused on philanthropy. Carnegie went to work at age 12 with just four years of formal education. By the time he retired from U.S. Steel at age 66, he was one of the richest men in the world. Though known for the tough tactics employed with striking workers during his business career, at his retirement he recalled a pledge he had made in his youth. He had promised himself that if he ever became rich, he would give away his wealth by the time he died. Carnegie substantially kept his pledge, and became one of the greatest philanthropists in history.

Howard Schultz, the CEO of Starbucks, has tried to integrate his belief that his work has a higher purpose into the way he does business. While growing up in the housing projects of Canarsie, Brooklyn, Schultz saw his father languish in poorly paying jobs. He vowed that "if I was ever in a position where I could make a difference, I wouldn't leave people behind." One of Starbucks' sources of competitive advantage has been a low turnover rate among workers, which may in part be attributed to the company's policy of offering full benefits to part-time employees.

Can You Make Your Work Fit Your Calling?

This is the question of the times, and it's a hard one to answer. If you are an expert—one who values mastery and control—and your mission is to become an aeronautical engineer, what do you do about your current job as a sales manager for a furniture company? You can't move from file cabinets to space shuttles overnight, and you may never breach the stratosphere at all. (There is a difference between callings and dreams.) But perhaps you can shift, over time, from sales manager to design engineer, or, if you have no design training, learn systems technology and use your new education to move from field sales to more technical work.

Some companies and industries—even very traditional ones—make it easier for employees to realign their work than others. Those who are still seeking the right match of work and values might do well to join companies like Cummins Engine, which rotates managers through jobs in several different specialties before asking them to settle down in one.

If, in the short term, you find yourself in a job that doesn't suit your abilities, values, and goals, consider the quaint idea that all work is a form of service. This humble, seemingly outdated notion has been revived in the customer service wave, which has recognized that the mission to serve the customer in all things is the key to organizational success. Such "enlightened" businesses tell employees that they are individual service units themselves. Other leaders inspire us with the idea that, even when work seems to lack meaning, the meaning is there—not in the work, but in the way we do it.

All work, Martin Luther King once said, is noble. Therefore, he suggested, "If you are going to sweep streets, do so like Beethoven composing symphonies." Or, as the founder of coffee retailer Starbucks likes to say, pour your heart into it.

For Further Reading

Built To Last: Successful Habits of Visionary Companies by Jerry Porras and James C. Collins (1994, HarperCollins)

Business as a Calling: Work and the Examined Life by Michael Novak (1996, The Free Press)

Pour Your Heart Into It: How Starbucks Built A Company One Cup at a Time by Howard Schultz (1997, Hyperion)

The Soul's Code: In Search of Character and Calling by James Hillman (1997, Warner Books)

Ultimate Rewards: What Really Motivates People To Achieve by Steven Kerr (1997, Harvard Business School Press)

Why Work? Motivating the New Work Force by Michael Maccoby (1995, Miles River Press)

Reprint U9712B

Speak to What Drives Them

• • •

Anne Field

Motivated employees are crucial to a company's success—this has never been more true than today, when margins are thin (or nonexistent) and economic recovery remains elusive. These hard bottom-line realities may also mean that managers can't rely as much as they might have in the past on using financial incentives to drive employee engagement.

So how do you keep people motivated and productive?

One answer lies in the concept of the career anchor, first developed some 30 years ago by Edgar Schein, a Sloan Fellows Professor of Management at the Massachusetts Institute of Technology. Schein says that people are primarily motivated by one of eight anchors—priorities that define how they see themselves and how they see their work.

In today's uncertain and turbulent business climate, pinpointing employees' career anchors is an especially useful tool because it allows you to do two crucial things: tailor your communication style to fit employees' individual needs and drive improved performance by choosing the most effective way to recognize and reward accomplishments.

The upshot: In a demanding environment where financial resources may be limited, you'll be able to make employees feel valued and motivated.

"If you use career anchors effectively, you'll turn your employees into high performers," says Linda Conklin, manager of alumni career services at the University of North Carolina and a former executive coach.

What are the eight anchors? They are:

1. TECHNICAL/FUNCTIONAL COMPETENCE. The key for a person with this career anchor is a desire to excel in a chosen line of work. Money and promotions don't matter as much as the opportunity to consistently hone a craft. While such professions as engineering and software design attract a lot of people with this particular bent, you can also find them just about anywhere, from the financial analyst excited by the chance to solve complicated investment problems to the teacher

happy to continually fine-tune classroom performance.

2. GENERAL MANAGERIAL COMPETENCE. Someone with this anchor is most closely allied with the traditional career path of the corporation. She is the polar opposite of the person for whom technical/functional competence is preeminent. She wants to learn how to do many functions, synthesize information from multiple sources, supervise increasingly larger groups of employees, and use her considerable interpersonal skills. What she craves is to climb the ladder, getting ever bigger promotions and salary increases.

3. AUTONOMY/INDEPENDENCE. Like Greta Garbo, individuals with this career anchor just want to be alone. They're most satisfied operating according to their own rules and procedures; they don't want to be told what to do. Freedom rather than prestige is their goal.

4. SECURITY/STABILITY. Employees with this career anchor value above all a predictable environment, one in which tasks and policies are clearly codified and defined. They identify strongly with their organization, whatever their level of responsibility.

5. ENTREPRENEURIAL CREATIVITY. The folks in this category want to create something of their own

and run it. They are, in fact, obsessed with the need to create and will become easily bored if they feel thwarted. As you'd expect, someone with this career anchor tends to start her own business, or at the least run something on the side while still keeping her day job.

6. SENSE OF SERVICE. The need to focus work around a specific set of values is the major issue for employees with this career anchor. But that doesn't just mean social workers, say, or nurses. It can also include anyone from a human resources specialist interested in affirmative action programs to a researcher working on developing a new drug. Money isn't the main event; it's the chance to focus on a particular cause.

7. PURE CHALLENGE. People with this career anchor seek ever-tougher challenges to conquer.

8. THESE FOLKS ORGANIZE THEMSELVES AROUND THEIR PRIVATE LIVES. Their most pressing concern is for their jobs to give them the freedom to balance those other concerns with their work.

Once you understand what each anchor is, you can determine the career anchor for each employee in your department. If you can't pinpoint the right area on your own, you can easily ask your staff to take a brief assessment, developed by Schein. Then you can take the next step and shape both how you communicate and how you recognize good performance in a way that fits each person's particular career anchor. Here are some guidelines:

Technical/Functional Competence

How to Communicate

"They want to be honored for what they know," says Jan Gamache, an executive coach who specializes in the development of senior executives and their teams. So you need to appeal to them as experts and try to see that others do the same. Gamache points to a highly respected engineer whose new CEO had failed to publicly acknowledge an appreciation for his preeminence in his field. The man had become very demoralized as a result and was considering quitting.

Also, in conversation with someone with a technical/functional competence anchor, if you know something about the field in question, display your knowledge. But if you don't, don't try to fake it. "They'll see through you immediately and will lose respect for you," says Bobbie Little, leader of the CEO Executive Coaching Division of DBM, a Connecticut–based outplacement firm.

Best Type of Recognition

These employees probably won't care that much if they can't get a raise. But they will become demoralized if

> Challenge those with the Entrepreneurial Creativity anchor with goals, not specific assignments. The more you let them figure you out, the happier they'll be.

they feel they can't keep refining their expertise or if they fear they won't be able to keep on being the best. "The worst possible thought for these people would be 'I've lost my edge,'" says Gamache. So make sure they can go to conferences, meetings, and other places where they're able to hone their craft and keep up with the latest developments.

General Managerial Competence

How to Communicate

The people in this group may be the easiest to talk to, thanks to their finely tuned interpersonal skills. They know how to lobby, they're good at politics, and they can read verbal and nonverbal cues. But in an atmosphere of limited resources, they also may be the hardest to please.

Because they're likely interested in how their performance fits into the organization as a whole, not just in the pure exercise of their expertise, make sure to discuss their work in terms of performance-based, bottom-line results. And ask their input on supervisory matters, so they feel they're stretching their managerial muscles.

Best Type of Recognition

These people really want more money and a promotion. Since you might not be able to provide those things, you need to look for other ways to enrich their jobs. For example, find big projects for them to supervise or invite them to attend important meetings. Send them to seminars and workshops where they'll learn to advance their skills. And see about giving them a more prestigious title.

In addition, look for secondary career anchors they might respond to. Conklin, for example, points to a hard-driving sales rep for a major hospital service provider whom she recently met. While he fell clearly into the general managerial area, he also showed signs of being in the lifestyle category, too. Unable to give him more money, management instead awarded him the opportunity to become a sales trainer. Result: He was able to dramatically cut back on his travel and spend more time with his family.

Autonomy/Independence

How to Communicate

These employees want to be on their own, so the less said, the better. Agree on a timetable for checking in with each other—and stick to it. And be prepared not to hear from them, even at the appointed time.

Little, for example, who supervises many autonomy-minded people, often finds it hard to schedule group conference calls. "At least one or two people usually don't make it," she says. "It's not that they're irresponsible, it's just that they have different priorities."

Best Type of Recognition

In the current tough climate, you may feel the need to interfere more than you might otherwise. Resist the temptation to do so. The most effective recognition you can give these people is the chance to "take the ball and run with it," says Barry Miller, instructor in management at Pace University's Lubin School of Business in New York City and an instructor in organizational management.

Security/Stability

How to Communicate

These days, people with this career anchor need to hear from you early and often. That means checking in frequently, so they're not left hanging. If there are rumors of cutbacks, keep communicating, even if you don't know the real story. Then come back again, even if nothing has changed.

Additionally, make a point of talking to them about the importance of life-long learning and keeping their skills up to date. If you don't urge them to take action, they won't.

Best Type of Recognition

You probably can't give them what they want: job security. But you can make the most of their loyalty to the organization and take steps to show appreciation for it, like taking them out to lunch or organizing a departmental picnic.

Entrepreneurial Creativity

How to Communicate

Encourage them to keep coming up with new ideas, no matter how wacky they may sound at first. And consistently ask them about projects they'd like to take on. Hold regular brainstorming sessions. These people tend to be highly enthusiastic, so try to match that upbeat quality, too. Challenge them with goals, not specific assignments, and leave them to get on with the job.

The more you let them figure out, the happier they'll be.

Best Type of Recognition

They also tend to be fairly self-centered. And they want money, not for its own sake, but as a visible sign they've accomplished something big. If you can't give them the money, you can provide public recognition as well as the reward they crave most the continued opportunity to create their own projects. Entrepreneurs can be extremely sensitive to slights and are not very good at taking criticism, so give them plenty of public praise when it's merited, and criticize them in private when necessary.

Sense of Service

How to Communicate

Don't just talk about the work. Focus on the aspect of the job that they most value. And look for projects that match their area of concern. Clarify the connection between the work and some loftier ideal. Let them know how they'll contribute to the greater good by doing the job at hand.

Best Type of Recognition

What they want most is to be able to continue working for their cause. By explicitly providing those opportunities, you'll give them what they need. You might also find that employees come up with unexpected ways to integrate their values into their work.

University of North Carolina's Conklin points to her assistant as one example. Conklin recently gave her a project—developing a seminar for students on how to dress for success. But because this assistant places great value on issues related to minorities, she made an effort to include a diverse group of models, in terms of size, shape, and color. Conklin plans on giving her assistant other projects that she can enrich with her particular value system.

Pure Challenge

How to Communicate

These people tend to be confrontational, often exuding a sense of urgency about the challenge of the moment and how to go about meeting it. As a result, "be prepared to push back," says DBM's Little. Insist on more explanation, when necessary, and on making sure the particular solution is the right one.

Raise the bar for success as high as you like; they'll thrive on it. Don't make anything too easy for them.

Best Type of Recognition

If you keep throwing challenges their way, they'll know they've done good work. When you see they're about to finish a project, try to find another for them to get started on immediately. Allow them a certain amount of time during the day to work on a particularly challenging assignment in addition to their regular duties.

For these people, the challenge is the reward, so don't go overboard with words of praise. Just get them going on the next job.

Lifestyle

How to Communicate

You need to be direct and to-the-point. Discuss what the employee needs and how best to organize schedules to accommodate his requests. Make sure the requirements of the job are clearly spelled out, together with the rewards for doing well and the penalties for doing poorly.

These people work to live, they don't live to work, so don't expect them to go beyond the basic requirements or job description. Make sure everything that you need from them is on the table.

Best Type of Recognition

Working out a flexible schedule is the most effective reward. Just as they don't expect to do more than the job's minimal requirements, they don't expect rewards beyond the salary. So give them the chance to maximize their nonwork hours when they do well and work efficiently. Get them to focus on getting the job done, not putting in a set number of hours, and reward them with time away from work.

Seek Employees' Input

Ultimately, you need to enlist your employees in your efforts. "Employees have to take the initiative to communicate with their managers about what's most important to them," says Conklin.

For example, she recently wrote out a wish list of 30 things she'd most like in her job, then sat down with her boss and hammered out a solution. (Her primary anchor is the autonomy/independence one.) Now, instead of doing the job she was hired for—conducting career workshops—she engages primarily in one-on-one counseling.

The bottom line, says Pace University's Miller: "People whose work is more meaningful are going to be more productive, even in tough times." By identifying employees' career anchors and communicating with them in a way that speaks to what's most important to them, you can help employees find that meaning in their work—and boost your unit's productivity, too.

Reprint C0309A

The Search for Meaningful Work

* * *

Loren Gary

Until recently, writes social critic Dinesh D'Souza, people the world over "derived a strong sense of satisfaction and purpose from providing for their families and sheltering their children from the ravages of necessity." But today, he writes in *The Virtue of Prosperity*, there are millions of people for whom "the struggle for existence has effectively ended."

So here's the question: why do *you* still go to work each day? Is it because your job provides the opportunity to be creative and to grow, use your power and influence productively, or exercise skills that you highly value? Because you believe the work your organization does contributes to the betterment of community and society? Or is it because you'd be at a loss to figure out what to do with yourself if you took your hand from the plow?

Here in the new millennium, do the labors of protecting your loved ones offer enough of what D'Souza calls a "horizon of significance," a conviction of "life's purpose as part of a moral order embedded in the cosmos"? Are you satisfied that the company you work for is making enough of a difference in the world? Or do you see things differently after September 11? Even though you still need to earn a living, do life's brevity and fragility make you set the bar higher for how the value of your days should add up?

Going far beyond the issue of achieving an optimal work-life balance, these questions get at the very meaning and end of work itself. They seem to be of greater moment at this juncture; people can't put them off as easily as before. In this respect, D'Souza's book and two others—*The Elephant and the Flea* by Charles Handy and *The Future of Success* by Robert Reich—provide a valuable service. Taken together, they offer insight into how broad economic patterns are reshaping roles and responsibilities throughout society, and guidance about how corporations and individuals can adapt.

Your Life as a Flea?

"Are you proud of your work?" Handy recalls his wife, Elizabeth, asking shortly after they were married many years ago. "It's all right, as work goes," he replied. "She looked hard at me, then said, 'I don't think I want to spend the rest of my life with someone who is prepared to settle for all right.'"

Given not only the prodigious economic successes of past years, but their side effects too, many people are no longer satisfied with work that merely gets the bills paid and the children educated. This restiveness, Handy writes, is appearing just as companies are becoming worried "that life outside the organization is becoming so

> Corporations take note: in Handy's view, it will be the 50-somethings, not the Gen Xers, who will transform the workplace.

attractive to free and independent spirits that there is a real danger of losing their best and most innovative people." The challenge for organizations, therefore, is to respond to employees' desire for more meaningful work, to be stand-up members of their communities, and to be profitable—all at the same time.

Handy doesn't presume to offer a one-size-fits-all answer to the question of what kind of work is more than just all right. Instead, he suggests that people frame the choice in terms of organizational affiliation: do you want to be an employee of the elephant (the large corporation) or one of its fleas (independent contractors)? "Work is hurriedly being reinvented. 'Employability' means 'think like an independent,'" he writes. "'Flexibility' means that no one can guarantee anything for long. Loyalty these days is first to oneself and one's future, secondly to one's team or project and only lastly to the organization."

Can individuals or organizations renew capitalism, making it at once more robust and more humane? If this transformation can be pulled off at all, Handy believes that individuals will be the primary agents of change. "Each of us has our own intellectual property," he says, "and will become better and better at guarding it and capitalizing on it." Free agency, life as a flea, will thus become more possible for a greater number of people. Of course, free agency is a rather moribund idea just now; in a recession, few people want to cut themselves loose from the relative security of corporate salaries and health and pension plans. But corporate elephants would do well to take notice all the same: in Handy's view, it will be the 50-somethings, not the Gen Xers, who will transform the workplace.

The flea existence becomes more attractive to people as they age, says Handy. "Many people spend their early twenties experimenting on their own, in small companies or in start-ups. They run for shelter to the organizations when they're getting into relationships, having children, taking out mortgages. They hang around in organizations for up to 20 years, then get frustrated." After the "proper job" ends (around age 55), most people will have to continue working. Some will leave the business world for the teaching and counseling fields, but many who stay will gladly trade higher salaries for greater flexibility. Even as they grow, companies must preserve an intimate, entrepreneurial environment that makes fleas want to affiliate with them. It's only by attracting such experienced talent that companies can hope to be competitive.

"Capitalism knows all about the means of wealth creation but is unclear about the ends, who or what that wealth should be for," Handy writes. To be a successful flea, you must provide that clarity for yourself—and for many, it comes only with age and experience. "You have to know what you want to do with your life, you've got to care, got to have a driving force, because your independent venture may not work," he says. "My first 10 years as a flea were not terribly rich. I was rushing about all the time." Without that underlying passion, he never would have persevered.

Recovering a Horizon of Significance

D'Souza takes a far rosier view of capitalism than Handy. "The movement from poverty to affluence represents a kind of moral progress," he writes. "It is a beneficial thing for individuals and societies because it expands the opportunity to act virtuously and help others." Thanks to capitalism, millions of people are now able to ask, "as only a handful of people in any given society have been able to in the past, What do I want to do with the rest of my life? What is my life for?" That they can ask these questions "is in and of itself a great moral achievement."

Nevertheless, D'Souza does acknowledge that "the gains of capitalism have come at a price." Increasingly, people are wondering whether there isn't more to the good life than material comfort. But now that the "community based on solidarity has been replaced by the society based on commerce," many no longer have a clue about what these other ingredients are. But casting one's glance backward, D'Souza writes, reveals other views of the good life "that were seriously offered, and seriously

> Thanks to capitalism, millions of people are now able to ask, as only the privileged few have been able to do in the past, What is my life for?

considered, in the ancient world." For instance: "the life dedicated to teaching, the life charged with political involvement, the life devoted to the service of others." These visions "cannot be recovered in the way they were advocated—as conceptions or blueprints for society as a whole—but they can supply us with personal horizons of understanding and significance."

The Search for Communal Solutions

Reich, the former U.S. secretary of labor, isn't satisfied with the recovery of a merely personal horizon of significance—he believes it can happen on a societal level. What's hindering this larger recovery? It's not that "enterprises are becoming colder-hearted, and executives more ruthless," he writes. Don't blame it on "an ethic of unbridled greed that seems to have taken hold in recent years." Rather, it comes down to regular folks like us. In our quest for the highest possible rates of return on our investments and the lowest possible prices for the goods and services we buy, we and consumers like us around the world unwittingly place enormous pressures on businesses to reduce the wages and benefits they pay to employees and to find "best buys among suppliers, who in turn must cut their costs in order to stay competitive." As the "pressure intensifies, institutional bonds are loosening."

Reich's insight here is that the separate conversations people find themselves having—one about "the wonders of the new economy," one about "the dangers and depredations of unfettered capitalism," and one about "the difficulties of achieving a balanced life in this new era"—must be linked together. Only then can communal answers to the problems identified be found.

For instance, employee benefits could be made fully portable. A kind of community insurance could be created, in which a region that loses, say, 5% of its economic base in the course of a year "would automatically get funds to help smooth the transition." Reich even goes so far as to suggest providing every 18-year-old in America "a financial 'nest egg' of, say, $60,000."

But one fact underlying the arguments in all three books remains: our questions about what gives work its value no longer presume conditions of scarcity. Economic success has enabled us to consider a higher order of questions. How we live in bad times and in good, and whether we choose to answer the questions individualistically or collectively, will occupy us well into this new century.

For Further Reading

The Elephant and the Flea: Reflections of a Reluctant Capitalist by Charles Handy (2002, Harvard Business School Press)

The Future of Success by Robert B. Reich (2001, Alfred A. Knopf)

The Virtue of Prosperity: Finding Values in an Age of Techno-Affluence by Dinesh D'Souza (2000, Simon & Schuster)

Reprint U0202D

Strengthening Personal Qualities

• • •

Motivated people demonstrate a set of distinctive personal qualities: they're optimistic while also being realistic about limitations, they take pride in their work, they build relationships of mutual trust with their managers, and they take steps to avoid burnout. You can help strengthen these qualities in your teams. For example, build trust by showing that you trust your people's skills and decision-making abilities, by keeping agreements, and by sharing information. Instill pride by explaining how your employees' work contributes directly to the company's bottom line. And resist the temptation to overload star performers who will "work themselves to death" to get the job done.

Staying Positive—Without the Illusions

• • •

Loren Gary

John Pierce was managing director of Merrill Lynch's retail brokerage office in Philadelphia from 1999 to mid-2003. For financial advisers, these were "the most difficult four years of their careers," he says. And that's not only because of the unprecedented market decline and corporate governance scandals of the period. Adding to the turbulence were charges that some analysts in the industry had inflated their estimates of companies to help their firms' investment bankers win clients.

Nevertheless, the natural optimism of his highest-performing brokers "made it easier for them to ignore all the bad news and gloomy indicators," says Pierce. Fixed in the belief that the dark clouds would soon be gone and that there was little they could do about the situation in the meantime, some brokers were "not as aggressive as they could have been in insisting that clients—many of whom were slow to acknowledge that the rapid rise in NASDAQ stock values was over—either change their asset allocations or find another investment adviser," says Pierce.

Recognizing that the brokers' ungrounded optimism was not going to produce the best results, Pierce put the brokers through training that addressed their tunnel vision and helped them see their situation in a more pragmatic light so that they could make better decisions. The training taught the brokers how to generate a wider range of possible causes of their situation, bring evidence to bear on them to determine which ones were the most realistic, and then craft plans for addressing the causes that they could do something about.

Of course optimism is vital to high performance—it fuels the ability to make creative connections between ideas, to convince others to take calculated risks and give their all to a project, and to persevere during sustained periods of corporate belt tightening. But optimism is truly effective only when rooted in reality. As Pierce's group discovered, you can teach yourself to temper your optimistic—and your pessimistic—tendencies to improve

> ## Optimism is truly effective only when rooted in reality.

your problem-solving ability. The operative skill here is resilience, which adds accuracy and flexibility to your habitual way of thinking about problems. Resilience is an inside-out skill: as you enhance your own personal resilience, your ability to apply it to such business situations as strategic planning and risk assessment also improves. The key to enhancing resilience is to develop a deeper appreciation for how beliefs influence emotions and behavior.

Beyond Motivation

Optimism's ability to stimulate innovation and enhance perseverance is well understood. But if you just try to instill a positive attitude in people without giving them the tools that will enable them to survive and thrive on their own, explains Cynthia Swall, an executive coach who works at Sprint's University of Excellence, then you're in a situation of continually having to reenergize their perspective. "We're not just looking for interventions that will help employees solve a particular problem, we're looking to help them continually adapt," she says. "Motivation and optimism alone are not going to create the sustainable change we're looking for."

So what is that vital other ingredient? An acknowledgment of reality. Noted management author Jim Collins highlights this in a psychological duality he calls the Stockdale Paradox in his book *Good to Great*. Named after Admiral Jim Stockdale, the highest-ranking U.S. military officer in the "Hanoi Hilton" prisoner-of-war camp during the Vietnam War, this paradox has to do with the ability to remain confident that you will prevail in the end while at the same time facing the harshest facts of your current reality. The optimists among the POWs had explanatory styles for understanding events that led them to focus on being freed soon. But the reality of the situation kept proving otherwise, and these POWs eventually broke under the stress of the disappointment.

Everyone has a distinct explanatory style, says University of Pennsylvania psychology professor Martin Seligman, author of the recent book *Authentic Happiness: Using the New Positive Psychology to Realize Your Potential for Lasting Fulfillment*. Styles vary along the three dimensions of personalization, permanence, and pervasiveness—an optimist, for example, possesses a "not me, not always, not everything" perspective.

An optimistic sales manager, therefore, would view a negative event, such as a 20% drop in sales during the most recent quarter, as not being her fault—she would point to the macroeconomic climate instead. She also wouldn't view the decline as being permanent (never going away) or pervasive (infecting all areas of her life). Instead, she would find temporary and specific causes: "The problem is the company's new pricing policy."

All explanatory styles have their shortcomings and distortions. For example, the sales manager's "not me" tendency can cause her to minimize or ignore her own contribution to the problem: "The decline in sales is not a reflection on my management style or skills, I just need to keep plugging away and things will turn around," she might conclude. By contrast, a manager with a stronger tendency to personalize "would be more likely to identify steps she could take to improve the situation," says Dean Becker, president and CEO of Adaptiv Learning Systems.

Teaching Resilience

Everyday distinctions between optimism and pessimism lack the nuance required to capture the dynamics involved in effective problem solving, Becker maintains, which is why Adaptiv emphasizes the concept of resilience instead. According to Adaptiv's vice president of research and development, Andrew Shatté, resilience involves seven factors:

1. Realistic optimism (which is born of an accurate identification of causes)

2. Causal analysis

3. Self-efficacy (having a conviction that you're able to solve problems)

4. Empathy

5. Emotion regulation

6. Impulse control

7. Reaching out (the ability to enhance the positive aspects of life).

Shatté, coauthor with Karen Reivich of *The Resilience Factor: Seven Essential Skills for Overcoming Life's Inevitable Obstacles*, says that by teaching people to be suspicious of their explanatory styles, "we help them develop greater flexibility in identifying and handling the causes of their problems." How? The work begins with a close examination of the connections linking adversity, beliefs, and consequences.

"We all have thoughts or beliefs that constantly run through our minds like ticker tape," says Becker. "These beliefs directly affect our emotions and behavior." When adversity strikes, an initial lack of information about its causes and likely outcomes tends to activate our explanatory styles and also any thinking traps we may regularly fall prey to. (The tunnel vision exhibited by the Merrill Lynch brokers is one example of a thinking trap; others include assuming that we know what other people are thinking and rushing to judgment before we have all the facts.)

In the face of adversity, Becker says, explanatory styles "can fuel ticker-tape beliefs that are simply not accurate, and therefore cause us to feel and act in inappropriate, nonresilient ways."

Slow down the ticker tape and identify both the *why* beliefs that have to do with the causes of the adversity and the *what-next* beliefs about its implications, advises Shatté. At Merrill Lynch, the training focused on improving brokers' causal analysis by bringing to light and then challenging the *why* beliefs that led the brokers to overlook steps they could take to regain a measure of control over their situation. Key elements of this process included teaching the brokers to capture their initial beliefs about what was causing their problems and then coaching them in consciously going against their explanatory style to generate alternative *why* beliefs. A final step was training them to use evidence for and against all their *why* beliefs to see which had the strongest factual basis.

The best way to deal with *what-next* beliefs is to map out the likely consequences. Case in point: A fairly young division president of a medical products company whose explanatory style was deemed by his boss and peers alike to be overly optimistic. To help the client gain greater perspective on potentially adverse situations, Minneapolis-based executive coach Chuck Bolton had him list the

Balancing Team Members' Explanatory Styles

One of a manager's most important tasks is balancing the optimistic and pessimistic tendencies in a group, says University of Pennsylvania psychologist Martin Seligman. "Generally, there's a division of labor that makes for sound functioning. Optimists tend to do best in jobs that call for high vision and initiative—for example, the sales, planning, and marketing functions. The financial, safety, and risk-assessment people are the pessimists." To the extent that you can, try to match a person's style with job responsibilities that take advantage of it. And use your knowledge of each member's style to help you evaluate his recommendation about new ventures under consideration. When, for example, the typically gung-ho member of your group is very wary about launching a new product, that's a sign worth paying special attention to.

possible negative implications of a situation he was facing and assign a likelihood to each. Next, the client fleshed out the most likely outcomes of these negative possibilities and developed solutions for them.

The same techniques that work for a person who minimizes adversity can also work for someone who habitually overreacts to it. The goal, says Adaptiv's Becker, is not so much to replace one explanatory style with another as it is to increase the flexibility and accuracy of your explanatory style. No matter what you're experiencing emotionally, it's important to ask, What is this belief buying me, and what is it costing me? "If it's leading you to miss areas in which you have a measure of control but aren't exercising it, or to burn resources on situations that you can't control," he says, "then you're missing a problem-solving opportunity."

Reprint U0309B

Working Like an Owner

• • •

Theodore Kinni

At General Motors' Car Assembly Plant in Wilmington, Delaware, there is a film that managers like to show when times get tough. Dating to 1991, the film opens with a GM executive saying that the plant will be closed in three years. There is no possibility of appeal, no chance the decision will be reversed, he says.

The next scene shows the plant's general manager. Maybe we can't save the plant, he declares, but we can make them feel really stupid for deciding to close it.

That's exactly what plant workers did. With nothing to gain, they built cars so well that dealers started specifically requesting them. Still slated to lose their jobs, the workers built cars so efficiently that they earned the right to a new-car launch. And when the time came to shut the plant down, headquarters had to refuse. The employees at Wilmington had made themselves too valuable to lose.

Jon Katzenbach, founder of the New York City-based consulting firm Katzenbach Partners and author of *Why Pride Matters More Than Money*, likes the story of the Wilmington plant because it communicates what he calls "institution-building pride."

In a tough economic environment, when there is little money for bonuses and a lot of concern about layoffs, Katzenbach says it becomes even more important to communicate with employees about the value of their work and reinforce the pride they take in it. This is not a recommendation to manufacture a false enthusiasm to gloss over problems. Speaking about and to employees' pride has to be authentic; employees will quickly sniff out managerial insincerity, and the manager's communication will backfire. As Donald N. Sull writes in *Revival of the Fittest: Why Good Companies Go Bad and How Great Managers Remake Them*, a new book about turnarounds, "successful managers exhibit a close alignment between what they commit to and who they are—and disconnects in that communication are disastrous."

To make a commitment to communicating about pride is to tap into a very powerful motivating force. Pride is an intrinsic, deeply seated human emotion, says Katzenbach, one that drives performance in the workplace in a number of ways, from creating and delivering a great product or service to winning a colleague's respect.

While the prestige and group identity that spring from working for a particular institution can be a motivating force for employees, it's pride in what they do—recognition of the intrinsic value of a job well done, whatever the job itself—that's the real powerhouse motivator because it speaks to employees' identity and self-worth.

Caring About Accuracy

Dave Thompson was appointed a measurement technician at Unocal's Van, Texas, oil field in 1993. He was responsible for making sure that the amounts of oil and natural gas pumped from the field were accurately recorded. This wasn't a challenge when it came to the oil, but gas was another matter. "Oil was always what buttered everybody's bread," he says, but no one seemed to care much about natural gas. In fact, only one Unocal field in North America had passed a natural gas measurement audit in years.

"We were selling seven to eight million cubic feet per day and I was responsible for it. I thought we should take a better interest in it," says Thomas. The problem was that although he was in charge of the machines that recorded the gas, he had no authority over the pumpers, the workers in the field who were directly responsible for keeping the recorders running 24 hours a day.

So Thompson appealed to their pride. "A lot of it was they just didn't know. What I did was I talked to them individually, and I explained why this should be done," he says. "They didn't always like it, but I explained to them that they ought to have pride enough in their jobs to learn about this piece of equipment and what it did."

He created a simple analogy to drive home the need for accurate measurement: If you were pumping gas into your car and the pump stopped registering at five gallons, even as the gas continued to flow, you wouldn't drive without paying for the whole tank. "This was about doing the right thing," says Thompson. "Pride and integrity go hand in hand with me."

Two years later, the company auditor gave the Van field the equivalent of a "B" grade on its gas audit. "This was like a fireworks display," remembers Thompson. "It reflected on the whole operation, and we took pride in the fact that the Van field and its employees were taking care of business." Two years after that, Van got the first "A" awarded by the company auditor in his 30 years at Unocal.

Now a production foreman, Thompson still lives and works in Van, just like always. "We are all blue-collar guys, we all like what we do, and we all feel confident and blessed," he says of himself and coworkers. "And I would take our group of 22 here and match them up against anybody in the industry."

Employees' Award-Winning Ideas

At Aetna, Rich Schlichting, a customer reporting and business operations manager, works closely with 16 people, almost all of them longtime employees, in his department. Those employees "own" the projects they work on, he says, because he assumes that they have the answers to most problems, if he will only listen.

"I've got tons of years of experience sitting right outside my cubicle. It only takes a little effort to stand up and walk outside and get everyone's opinion," he says.

The Wellsprings of Pride

It is fairly easy to build pride when you work for a peak-performing organization, such as Southwest Airlines or the U.S. Marine Corps; people are proud to be affiliated with winners. But where do you turn when it isn't so easy to take pride in your company's current performance?

There are many sources of pride, says Jon Katzenbach. Try appealing to:

Pride in colleagues. Microsoft was vilified as a monopoly, but its employees continued to take great pride in being part of a workforce heralded as one of the most intelligent and hard-working in the world.

Pride in heritage. Aetna has had a few tough years, but employees could still lean on the company's 150-year heritage of helping their policyholders deal with disaster.

Pride in producing a great product or service. GM's Wilmington plant was slated for closure, but employees took pride in proving their ability to turn out high-quality cars.

Pride in community. After more than 70 years of production, Unocal's Van field doesn't produce as much as it once did, but its workers still take pride in their contributions to their hometown's quality of life.

Pride that comes from earning the boss's respect. People will work hard to earn the respect of a leader they admire. Managers who communicate the pride they feel in their employees help perpetuate the pride-building cycle.

When he first started the job, Schlichting realized that there were a couple of people who were de facto leaders in the group. "There were two people who everybody looked to for answers. So, I focused on them initially—gaining their trust and asking them what we could do to make things better."

When he receives good ideas, Schlichting lets the employees implement them. "Giving a project out gives them a little more pride," he says. "They've got ownership, and they want to make sure that it gets done." He makes sure that employees are recognized for their ideas within the department during small recognition ceremonies, like a quarterly lunch. And when appropriate, he nominates them for greater honors, such as Aetna's corporate recognition program, the Pathfinder Award.

"I know there are some managers who don't want to take the time to fill out a simple form," he says, "but it really doesn't take that much effort."

Five employees in Schlichting's department have won Silver Awards with a $300 prize, and two have gone on trips to Florida afterward to compete at the second (Gold) level of the three-level program. One of them went on to win the annual Platinum Award and its $5,000 prize for the implementation of his idea to deliver the department's monthly claim reports electronically to self-insured customers.

"It was his idea, he ran with it, and he took ownership," says Schlichting. "There was no funding for the project, and it was all done within the unit. Everybody wanted this to be successful, and everybody stayed extra hours to make sure it was done properly." The electronic reports get to customers up to two weeks faster than mailed copies do and save Aetna $300,000 annually.

"I inherited a good crew," says Schlichting. "They take pride in their work. They realize that I do listen and I do take their advice, and I do recognize and reward people who are doing a good job."

Pride in Numbers

As Unocal's Thompson and Aetna's Schlichting show, a strong bond between manager and employee is an essential element in pride building.

"Relationship, trust, and pride are all intertwined," says General Motor's Rick Sutton, the site manager for two Saginaw, Michigan, power-train plants employing 3,000 people. "The way I look at it is, in order to build pride, you have to have trust, and in order to have trust, you have to have a relationship. So you've got to figure out how to connect and spend time with people."

But how do you establish a personal connection when you manage thousands of employees who may well be working in different locations and on different shifts? One way that Sutton makes the connection is through videotaped messages. He recognizes the impersonal nature of a taped message, but he overcomes that by using an "unscripted fireside chat. It's 'Here's what we are doing well,' with a lot of thank-yous and kudos and pointing out wins and successes, and then talking about how we need to redirect energy into what comes next."

Sutton uses the videos to issue an invitation. "There are 140 teams in this organization, and I tell them that if any team would like to talk to me further, I will come to their team meeting any day, any time, on their turf." The employees do respond; Sutton averages one team meeting per week.

The meetings are where Sutton gets beyond metrics. "When you sit in the front office and let the layers of management filter out what is really going on in your plant, it is very different from meeting with these guys and listening to what they are telling you." Just as important is responding to the expressed needs. "They might give you more than one chance, but not many more. But once you make that connection and people understand that you care about their problems and you are there to help, the energy in the organization is amazing."

It has worked at Saginaw. Since 1999, the employees have delivered $20 million or more each year in cost savings, with capital expenditures of less than $500,000 total.

"We're talking $80 million out of a $400 million cost structure," says Sutton, "and it isn't that amazing, once you really understand the talent, ability, and power of proud people."

Reprint C0308A

Trust

How to Build It, Earn It—and Reestablish It When It's Broken

• • •

Trust may be just as important a determinant of economic prosperity as physical capital, if only because it allows people in organizations to work together more effectively. "A high-trust society can organize its workplace on a more flexible and group-oriented basis," writes Francis Fukuyama in his book *Trust*, "with more responsibility delegated to lower levels of the organization."

But trust isn't exactly something you can buy off the shelf—nor can managers content themselves with understanding it on a theoretical level. If trust is to be "the great enabler of the new economy"—to quote Russell J. Campanella, chief people officer at NerveWire—managers must be able to wring tangible results from it.

At Boeing, vice president Mary Armstrong is attempting to do just that. "There have been a great deal of changes in how we provide our services," she explains. The pace of change was making it hard for people to respond and still feel comfortable in their jobs. A lot of people were becoming disengaged—everyone was still working hard, but our overall effectiveness was only 30%–40%." Together with a task force of 35 volunteers from all levels, she and manager Barry Foster have identified trust as one of the drivers of improved performance. And they've embarked upon a year-long effort to do something about it.

The first step has been to develop a granular understanding of how trust functions in the organization. To do this, the task force is using a tool for assessing trust developed by organizational-systems experts Michelle and Dennis Reina. The instrument asks respondents to rate how closely each of 48 statements matches the situation in their own company. Sample statements include: "If employees have a concern or issue with an individual, they speak directly to that person" and "Management receives constructive feedback without getting defensive." The tabulated responses produce measures for three key components:

1. communication trust (or trust of disclosure), the extent to which employees are willing to share information;

2. contractual trust (or trust of character), em-

ployees' faith in one another's integrity and ability to keep agreements; and

3. competence trust (or trust of capability), employees' respect for one another's abilities.

The more these components are in evidence, the more likely you are to have what the Reinas call *transactional trust* between managerial and nonmanagerial employees.

After taking the test themselves, task force members will administer it to another pilot group of volunteers. From there, they'll have a much clearer sense of the areas that need to be addressed first. For example, if managers score low on the competence trust scale, it may be an indication that they are micromanaging, not giving direct reports the freedom to do their jobs.

Down in the trenches, trust can be remarkably hidden and mercurial. It seems to be least in evidence, notes consultant and author Robert Shaw, where it's talked about the most. Before you can receive it, you have to be willing to give it. Try too earnestly to foster it, and your efforts can backfire, instilling suspicion among employees. What follows is some concrete advice for dealing with an admittedly squishy subject.

1: Develop Your Own Capacity for Trust First

"The starting point of a trusting relationship is your own relationship with yourself," declares Michelle Reina.

"Your readiness to trust in yourself influences your beliefs and perceptions." When you believe that you are dependable and reliable, you have confidence when dealing with the unknown. Your ability to trust others grows with your own ability to trust yourself. This creates a positive feedback loop, because others' willingness to put their trust in you is influenced by their perception that you see yourself as trustworthy. CEO Paul Walsh of Diageo has invented an acronym for this self-fulfilling managerial philosophy: API, or the assumption of positive intent. "I try to show people that if anybody disagrees or has a violently opposed argument or fundamentally thinks another person is wrong, that the basis for their assumption is positive intent for the good of the organization." When you're confident of your own motives and capabilities, you're likely to attribute good intentions to others.

People have varying capacities for trust, Reina continues. In its most simplistic forms, trust can be overly idealistic and undifferentiated—for example, a person who makes blanket generalizations about others. In their book, *Trust & Betrayal in the Workplace,* the Reinas offer exercises that can help you develop a more nuanced capacity for trust.

For instance, think about a colleague—someone you don't have much contact with, but who your friends say is untrustworthy. The next time you interact with him, stop and take notice. What was your attitude toward him? How did you come across? Make a point of getting

How to Heal from Betrayal

1. Observe what has happened. Pay attention to the thoughts telling you you've been taken advantage of or sold out.
2. Honor the loss you've experienced by allowing all the negative feelings to surface—instead of dismissing them hastily, use them as diagnostic guides.
3. Reach out to others who can help you deal with your feelings.
4. Reframe the experience in a larger context: ask yourself what lessons the betrayal can teach you about yourself and others. This will help you achieve a measure of objectivity and detachment.
5. Analyze how you could have handled the situation differently, and take responsibility for the role you played in the process.
6. Forgive yourself and the person who betrayed you.
7. Decide how you'll act differently the next time a similar situation occurs, then let go and move on.

to know the person better—his skills and strengths as well as some details about his personal life. What is your attitude toward him now? Was your original impression accurate? How has your interaction changed?

2: Build Trust Behaviorally and Incrementally

A capacity for trust enables you to take the first step in trusting another. But your trust must be validated by the other person's actions if it is to grow. "We trust those who demonstrate that they are worthy of it," writes Shaw. For instance: a fairly new employee who's performed well in an adjunct role on an important project. "You may now trust his competence and character enough to give him more independence on the next big assignment," says Dennis Reina. "But it could be entirely appropriate for you not to disclose the company's most closely held proprietary secrets to him at this stage."

As trust grows, managers become more willing to give their reports greater responsibilities—and their reports become more willing to accept or even ask for such responsibilities. But showing confidence in someone by giving him a new challenge doesn't require you to jettison your standards. Patrick Kelly, CEO and president of PSS World Medical describes how, years ago, he promoted Jim Boyd to manage the fast-growing central region division of the company—a job that Boyd himself says he wasn't prepared for. After missing his numbers for several months, Boyd says that he began to lose his managerial confidence and make poor decisions. Kelly tried to support Boyd yet insisted that he still make his numbers. When Boyd failed to do so, Kelly removed him from the position.

At the time, Boyd remembers, Kelly's action "really devastated me." But looking back, he feels that he was held accountable but not punished for failing to deliver his numbers, and because of that he was able to learn some important lessons. To borrow Shaw's terminology, Kelly simultaneously demanded results, expressed true concern for Boyd, and maintained his own integrity (the alignment between what he said and what he did). He recalibrated his trust in Boyd without lowering the expectations for the job—and also without making Boyd feel that he had completely lost Kelly's confidence. Boyd's next position—selling large capital equipment to doctors—carried significant responsibility. PSS later capitalized on Boyd's work by creating a diagnostic division that grew into a $200 million unit—with Boyd at the head.

3: Tackle Betrayal Head-on

Psychologist James Hillman maintains that you never fully understand how to trust until you've experienced betrayal and have intentionally worked your way through it. The Reinas' experience in the corporate world bears this out. "We've encountered numerous CEOs who won't trust others until they've proved themselves by passing some specific 'test' the CEO created," says Dennis Reina. "Sometimes that's a sign that the CEO has been burned in the past." His capacity for trust has diminished as a result.

Michelle Reina defines betrayal as the "breach of trust,

or the perception of such." There are gradations of betrayal, depending on the intentions of the betrayer and the impact of the behavior. Sabotaging the corporate database would constitute a major intentional betrayal; repeatedly showing up late for work, a minor unintentional betrayal.

The most serious violations of trust often occur at the hands of the most trusted colleagues or direct reports. "The greater the loyalty and involvement, the greater the betrayal," writes Hillman. But the Reinas add that ongoing minor betrayals often represent the most immediate concern. "One of the most frequent examples is micro-management," says Michelle Reina. "It makes the employee feel that the manager doesn't trust her competence."

Most people respond to betrayal with denial—they keep their eyes wide shut. But the Reinas' advice for handling it is to be exquisitely alert to what's going on inside you.

When managers feel betrayed, their self-trust *and* their ability to trust others wither. And the cumulative effects can be crippling: the company's ability to innovate and to respond to change falls off noticeably. So healing from workplace betrayal isn't important just on a personal level—it's essential to the health of the organization.

For Further Reading

Trust: The Social Virtues and the Creation of Prosperity by Francis Fukuyama (1995, Free Press)

Trust & Betrayal in the Workplace: Building Effective Relationships in Your Organization by Dennis S. Reina and Michelle L. Reina (1999, Berrett-Koehler Publishers)

Trust in the Balance: Building Successful Organizations on Results, Integrity, and Concern by Robert Bruce Shaw (1997, Jossey-Bass)

Reprint U0009A

The Rise of Hyperarchies

• • •

Loren Gary

Frustrated with the way that a traditional top-down organization's need for control seems to stifle the ability to adapt, innovate, and take calculated risks, businesses have been experimenting with alternative structures for decades. Now a form of economic organization known as a *hyperarchy* is receiving attention because of its ability to unleash rather than constrain the intrinsic motivation of employees.

A hyperarchy is "a large-scale, self-organizing community that sets free unusually high degrees of energy and engagement—despite the lack of clear or direct economic payoff for participants," says Boston Consulting Group partner Philip Evans. For example, Toyota's famously lean supply chain has evolved over the past two decades into a self-organizing community that relies, at times, on voluntary contributions almost unthinkable in a conventional business. The significance of this was brought into high relief in 1997, when a fire at a plant of Aisin Seiki, one of Toyota's tier-one suppliers, destroyed the automaker's sole source of p-valves, a key component in brakes.

Since Toyota intentionally maintained low inventories, the entire supply chain quickly ground to a halt. But the tier-one suppliers decided to improvise the production of p-valves using whatever general-purpose machinery was available. Each tier-one supplier mobilized its tier-two suppliers; they, in turn, mobilized their tier-three suppliers, in a nested, self-replicating fashion. There was no up-front haggling about how people or companies would be reimbursed. Instead, ad hoc teams formed across firms; Aisin Seiki freely shared its blueprints, raw materials, and any specialist machinery that had survived the fire. Other groups stepped forward to "traffic-cop" the new sets of logistics. Ten days after the fire, more than 60 firms were producing enough p-valves to get the entire system running again—thanks to the initiative of a number of companies, only one of which was Toyota.

Perhaps the best-known hyperarchy is the Linux project, part of the broader open-source software movement in which program source code is given away to volunteers who help fix bugs and design new features. Linux operating systems have generated huge economic value, says Evans: they drive more than 50% of all embedded devices and have more of the server operating systems market than Microsoft's Windows NT. But this value doesn't show up in the GNP because it accrues as a free benefit to users.

The success of such self-organization "flies in the face of many economists' assumptions about self-interest," says Evans, coauthor of *Blown to Bits: How the New Economics of Information Transforms Strategy*. In a conventional market, the primary transaction currency is the contract—the system of negotiating, paying, and litigating, when necessary, to enforce agreements. Moreover, an asymmetry of information—having access to data that another participant does not—can often give you bargaining power.

Hyperarchies, by contrast, use simple rules to increase transparency and symmetry of information. When all Linux programmers can pretty much see what everyone else is doing, everyone has an incentive to reciprocate when others share information with them; in the course of such sharing, participants build strong reputations throughout the community. Reciprocity and reputation thus work together to establish trust as the primary transaction currency in a hyperarchy. So when the fire occurred at the Aisin Seiki plant, Toyota's suppliers didn't feel the self-protective need to negotiate their compensation first before jumping in to solve the problem. High degrees of transparency and symmetry of information throughout the supply chain had made trust the principal medium of exchange. The suppliers trusted that Toyota would do right by them in the end (which it did).

For challenges that place a premium on innovation and adaptability, hyperarchic organizations of individuals can generate higher levels of energy and engagement than top-down structures because they allow participants to largely choose their own tasks, operate at their own pace, and derive satisfaction from the work itself. This intrinsic motivation combines with the foundation of trust to create a virtuous circle: the more that participants in a hyperarchy are recognized as trusted contributors, the greater their motivation.

Reprint U0403F

High-Performance Prison

• • •

Jennifer McFarland

A recent International Labour Organization study found that one in 10 workers suffers from stress, anxiety, depression, or burnout. But the blame cannot be pinned solely on downsizing or the pace of business. Employees—especially top performers—are often complicitous in their own exhaustion. Paradoxically, extraordinary achievement can give rise to fears that lead to burnout.

To understand burnout you have to take into account "the addictive, almost erotic, appeal that deep and obsessive involvement in a task can have," writes consultant Tom DeMarco in *Slack*. Highly motivated individuals are most susceptible, notes Southern Illinois University assistant professor Jo Ellen Moore. They "often have strong self-management skills and need little supervision; they can be counted on to know what needs to be done and do it." Not surprisingly, managers tend to overload these star employees, who "will work themselves to death to get it done." Adds DeMarco: "The high, the narcotic of gonzo overindulgence, and the associated fatigue all combine to reduce the individual's mental capacities." And if "they have any capacity left at all, they will use it to conceal the burnout, or at least to try to do so."

Psychologist Steven Berglas develops the addiction metaphor further in his book *Reclaiming the Fire*. Successful people cause their own demise, he argues, by believing that everything will be all right—if only they can land the next project or clinch one more sale. But the expected psychological satisfaction almost never materializes. Success becomes a drug, and star performers constantly feel the need to score. "Once you attain a goal, you adapt to the high and the buzz wears off," Berglas explains. "Then the feeling of 'been there, done that' creeps in. Now what? You need higher and higher levels of the drug to get the desired psychological effect."

Underlying almost every symptom of what Berglas calls "Supernova Burnout" is "the feeling that the material, self-esteem, and interpersonal rewards accrued from success will be jeopardized by ongoing assessments of one's capabilities," he explains. "Consequently, in what should be a sublime afterglow following achievement, many careerists discover that they are blocked from initiating constructive changes by what psychologists call risk aversion." This fear of taking on new challenges manifests itself as *encore anxiety* ("What do I do next to top my last success?"), *entrepreneurial arson* (intentionally creating problems in order to relieve the boredom), and *self-handicapping behavior* (externalizing responsibility for potential failure by turning to drugs or alcohol).

Dealing with success-induced risk aversion is more a matter of "reconfiguring your gestalt" than of completely reinventing yourself, says Berglas. "Until you can see yourself as more than the sum of the component assets that can trap you on an identity-fostering-but-frustrating career path, you are vulnerable to all-or-

Are You a Candidate for Supernova Burnout?

Look at the following list of adjectives:

___Single-minded	___Unremitting
___Persevering	___Monomaniacal
___Self-reliant	___Zealous
___Assiduous	___Indefatigable

If you're over 40 and believe that at least four of these terms apply to you, then you're a "slam-dunk, guaranteed case of Supernova Burnout in the making," writes Steven Berglas in *Reclaiming the Fire*.

nothing thinking about the consequences of introducing challenge, innovation, or change into your job."

To avoid becoming root-bound, repot your career periodically. If the economy makes it difficult to do that, make time for activities that invigorate you mentally. If your "self-esteem has multiple infusions of positive feedback and satisfaction," Berglas explains, "it is more stable, less threatened by the potential of failing at innovation and change."

For Further Reading

Reclaiming the Fire by Dr. Steven Berglas (2001, Random House)

Slack: Getting Past Burnout, Busywork, and the Myth of Total Efficiency by Tom DeMarco (2001, Broadway Books)

Reprint U0106D

Fostering Commitment Beyond Just the Job

• • •

When you motivate your people to excel, their energy and creativity ripple across the entire organization. Motivated employees make others feel fully engaged in the work at hand and inspire others to focus on possibilities rather than problems. They also feel responsible for entire business processes, not just their own tasks. And they work to "unstick" knowledge—to transfer best practices across units and functions so that the company as a whole can benefit. You can foster commitment beyond a task or job—by clarifying the company's fundamental objectives and ways of measuring progress toward those goals, challenging employees to identify opportunities to leverage existing knowledge, and ensuring that people understand how all the parts of the organization (R&D, marketing, customer service, finance, etc.) work together.

How to Energize Colleagues with Wayne Baker

• • •

Power and influence in today's companies have less to do with employees' positions on the organizational chart and more to do with their ability to energize others in their organizational networks, says Wayne Baker. Groundbreaking research by Baker, Rob Cross (assistant professor at the University of Virginia's McIntire School of Commerce), and Andrew Parker (then research associate at the IBM Institute for Knowledge-Based Management) was able to measure the long-noted influence that energizing relationships have on performance.

1. How were you able to link energizing behavior to performance?

We combined network analysis with survey questions that asked respondents to rate the energizing or de-energizing effect of interacting with each of the people in their organization. That enabled us to create an energy map that showed where the pockets of energy were and also where the de-energizing interactions were in the organization.

When we compared the maps against the respondents' annual performance ratings, which were based on objective measures of project outcomes and customer feedback, we found that the more people you energize, the higher your performance rating, and vice versa.

Someone who is energizing elevates the performance of other people around her. They feel more creative when they're working with her; they're more likely to work hard on her behalf and to devote discretionary time to her projects.

2. What distinguishes energizers?

Energizers do five things very well. They create a compelling vision by focusing on possibilities rather than current or past problems. They help others feel fully engaged. And while they're doing that, energizers are also learning from their colleagues. Energizers are goal-oriented but flexible about how to get there—they allow progress to occur in unexpected ways. Finally, energizers speak their mind, maintaining integrity between their words and actions. This influences others' willingness to believe that the goal is worthy and attainable.

3. Are energizing behavior and high-energy behavior the same thing?

A high-energy or charismatic person generates what psychologists call *high-arousal emotions* in others. But energizing behavior is about letting other people know they matter—for example, when someone comes into your office to speak with you, you devote your physical presence and undivided attention to that person. Even a shy person can be energizing in this way.

People don't have to initially like the leader of a project in order to be energized. The ability to energize isn't a function of personality; it has to do with the behaviors you exhibit in your interactions with others.

4. Couldn't energizing behavior lead to groupthink?

An energizer isn't a cheerleader or a wild-eyed optimist; he simply focuses on the opportunities rather than the constraints. When energizers hear a suggestion they disagree with, instead of dismissing it outright, they'll search for what's good in that suggestion. De-energizing people tend to be more negative, focusing on all the reasons why you can't do something.

To me, de-energizing behavior is the more likely cause of groupthink. People who are de-energizing often possess valuable knowledge and alternative views of things. But because of their de-energizing behavior, these people become isolated: their expertise and knowledge go untapped. By contrast, energizing people are more likely to increase the flow of information—including divergent points of view—throughout the organization.

5. How do you turn de-energizers into energizers?

First you need to create awareness, then follow it up with diagnosis. The supervisors at the petrochemical company we studied were aghast when they saw the network charts diagramming their de-energizing effect on others. That kind of data is hard to argue with; it prodded the supervisors to analyze their behavior and discover that they had been micromanaging.

When you're analyzing your behavior, look at how you use your own expertise: Do you destroy others' energy in your haste to find a solution or demonstrate your knowledge? Do you have a tendency to force others to come around to your way of thinking? Also, when disagreement arises, do you focus on the individual rather than on the issue at hand?

Reprint U0407C

What You Can Learn from Open-Book Management

● ● ●

John Case

Every company, so it seems, gives at least lip service to the concept of empowerment these days. Employees are expected to manage their own work, serve on problem-solving teams, even schedule their own time and track their own hours. Plenty of companies have found that empowerment leads to improved performance. As the saying goes, who knows how to do a job better than the person doing it?

The potential trouble with most empowerment schemes, however, is that people may focus only on their own job or their team's, and not on the performance of their company or business unit. At best this leads to a myopic concentration on individual tasks. At worst it leads to buck-passing and finger-pointing. ("We got the product down to shipping but they didn't get it out the door.") Empowered employees need to learn to take responsibility for whole business processes, not just for the parts of the process that they happen to work in.

One route to responsible empowerment is a system called open-book management. In it, companies "open the books" to employees throughout the organization, and, in a series of systematized steps, educate them so that they can see the same big picture that more senior executives do. With that shared understanding, employees are better equipped to tailor their actions to the requirements of the day. Since the mid-1980s companies have been finding that open-book management helps people solve problems faster, stay on track, innovate more quickly, and generate earnings. Springfield ReManufacturing, an open-book pioneer that competes in the gritty business of engine remanufacturing, has grown a consistent 15 percent each year for the past decade. Physician Sales & Service (PSS), a $600-million distributor of medical supplies to doctors' offices, has grown to become the largest company of its kind. And the open-book R.R. Donnelley & Sons printing plants are among the top-performing units in the corporation.

At root, open-book management relies on only three simple ideas:

People work better when they know what's going on.

In open-book companies, employees learn to under-stand the business's fundamental objectives and met-rics. They learn how their jobs affect their unit's results, and how the unit affects the company's performance. Warehouse workers and customer-service clerks aren't expected to become CPAs, but they are expected—and are taught—to understand budgets, forecasts, P&Ls, and many of the other report cards by which companies gauge their accomplishments.

People who know their company's objectives and metrics can take responsibility for their own work.

In companies of yore, it might have been only the man-ager who worried if a factory's shipments were lower than plan or a store's average sale per customer was down 10 percent. In open-book companies, everybody sees these numbers—and everybody shares responsibility for bettering them. So people tend to think a lot about how to get the work done better, faster, and cheaper.

People need a stake in their company's success.

Employees of most companies make the same money no matter how the company does. They're hired hands.

Open-book companies ask their employees to think and act as if they owned the place, and they structure compensation accordingly. Typically, they'll pay sizable bonuses whenever the business hits its financial targets. Many have generous employee stock-ownership plans as well.

These principles are part of a management system, and so reinforce each other. At PSS, the medical supplies distribution company, employees of every branch see the facility's operating P&L—actual numbers compared to plan—at monthly meetings. To help them understand these numbers, PSS sponsors customized question-and-answer games based on the TV shows *Family Feud* and *Jeopardy,* which can occasion a good deal of hilarity. Any number that is off plan provokes a round of discussion and brainstorming about what employees can do to get it back on track. PSS employees have strong incentives to watch these numbers closely: Nearly all are shareholders. They'll get bonuses potentially worth thousands of dollars apiece if the branch hits or exceeds plan while meeting certain other financial goals.

Opening the Books
in "Closed" Organizations

Sounds good. But what's the gap between theory and practice? CEOs and small-business owners can decide to share the financials, set up a new bonus plan, and do everything else involved in creating an open-book company. But what if you're a manager running a department or business unit in a large corporation? You may not have the authority to decide who can see key numbers. You may not even see them yourself. You can't suddenly revamp the compensation system or ask employees to assume responsibilities not in the union contract. Changes like these take time and resources, not to mention a lot of support from the powers that be.

But that doesn't mean that the ideas behind open-book management can't be useful to you and your organization. Indeed, you can apply some key open-book principles even in the most conventional of companies. And you may find that applying them boosts people's performance notably, even compared to results organizations may get when they go whole hog.

How can you apply these principles in a not-so-open organization? The secret is to extract the basic ideas, get people started in ways that won't threaten anybody—and then, ever so gently, push the edges of the envelope.

Supplying Information in Context

Most companies these days provide employees with reams of data. Customer-service reps know how long the average caller is on hold. Machine operators see charts showing size variations and defect rates. Walk into nearly any plant or office and you'll find scoreboards and tally sheets of many sorts, including electronic ones. The employees of Sony Display Device San Diego, for example, can check output numbers, inventory discrepancies, and other figures on the company's intranet.

Simply posting numbers in this manner is sometimes a step toward higher performance. People gauge themselves against the standard (or against yesterday's performance) and want to do better. Still, it doesn't take long for this particular game to get old. If you don't know what the numbers mean or why they matter, it's hard to stay too excited about improving them.

Open-book companies don't just put numbers up on the wall; they show why the numbers matter by linking them to the big picture. Say a unit's financial goal is to boost earnings by 10 percent in the course of a year. The plan calls for increasing shipments eight percent, maintaining gross margins, and reducing SG and A expense. That plan, in turn, provides every department and work area with a variety of critical numbers—numbers that matter if the unit is to achieve its goal. Suddenly weekly shipment levels take on a new meaning. So do seemingly trivial numbers like postage or telephone expense. People watch them all, because they're working together toward the same objective.

Organizations can do something of this sort even without open books. For example, what is your department's or unit's key operating goal? To produce or sell a certain quantity? To serve a specific number of customers while holding expenses at budget? These are significant goals, and it's not hard for people to understand why they might be important. A scoresheet tallying progress toward big goals will generate more interest than a scoresheet that only tallies progress toward smaller objectives. What's more, the big goal provides the context that gives the smaller objectives meaning.

Getting into a Huddle

How to cultivate this way of thinking? An approach pioneered by Springfield ReManufacturing Corp. and other open-book companies is huddling. The sports-minded term derives from SRC's moniker for its open-book system, The Great Game of Business. In SRC's series of huddles, every department in the organization works off an annual plan or budget. Departments get together weekly or biweekly to review their performance against plan goals. A representative from the department takes those numbers to a plant-wide or company-wide meeting, where the numbers for that level are assembled. Then the consolidated numbers are distributed back to departments and work areas so people can see how the whole business unit is doing.

SRC's numbers are mainly financial. But informing employees so they understand the key levers and areas that will help bring a company to goal can be accomplished even if the financial books aren't open. How many customers were served? How far off budget are we on expenses? How do shipments compare with plan? If your superiors are worried about sharing numbers, you can substitute percentages for dollar figures. But do include numbers from the whole company or business unit, not just one department.

The continuous feedback has two salutary effects. One is that it reminds people week in and week out that they are part of a whole—and that what matters is the performance of that whole, not just of their own team. More important, it forces people to manage their numbers. Units that are off plan know that they're letting down the rest of the organization, so they begin trying to anticipate problems before they arise. They're empowered—not simply to manage their own work area, but to do what the company needs them to do.

Giving People a Stake in Success

An open-book bonus system is a powerful incentive program. It provides substantial rewards to people who better their performance, and it allows employees to track their progress toward the bonus over the course of the year. You may not be able to set up such a bonus system right away. Still, managers can use a variety of tools and techniques to tie a unit's performance to compensation:

- Large companies usually have some sort of employee stock-ownership plan: an employee stock-option plan, or a stock-purchase plan coupled to a 401(k). Any company's share value depends partly on the performance of each business unit. Employees know that. They can be encouraged to become shareholders, and they can be reminded of their interest in the long-term health of the company.

- Many companies also have profit-sharing programs. These programs may have nothing to do with the performance of your business unit or department, but people understand that high performance ultimately contributes to the payout from profit-sharing plans. People also know that better-performing units tend to get rewarded more than underperforming units over time.

- Pride is a form of compensation, and people often take it as seriously as money. How does your operation stack up against others in the company? Others in the industry? Open-book companies challenge people to be the best, and show on the scoreboard how they stack up against their competitors, internal or external.

- Small rewards are sometimes as meaningful as big ones. Did the office hit its customer-service target? Were the plant's monthly shipments 10 percent over plan? At some companies, managers buy pizza for everybody when plan goals are exceeded. Others hold a drawing for two tickets to a show. Some companies pay spot bonuses of $25 per person.

Pushing the Envelope

When first introduced to the idea of open-book management, many companies object, often out of self-protectiveness. "We can't release financial data because we're publicly traded" is the most common response. In fact, however, a lot of open-book companies are public, including PSS. And companies can share business-unit and department performance numbers while restricting access to consolidated financial data. Some organizations flinch at the thought that the union might take advantage to press for more money. This is a pragmatic concern, but the principles of open-book management lend themselves to approaching the union to explore the idea of cooperating to design pay-for-performance compensation plans.

The most serious concern—"Our competitors will learn our numbers"—demonstrates the extent to which managing with open books is a balancing act. There is always key data that companies must protect. But open-book companies find they can share much more information with employees than they once thought safe. And again, they are dedicated to the idea that employees can't work effectively in the dark. Organizations that have implemented open-book management find that such objections evaporate when the results are in. Often, in fact, open-book management spreads through a company like a wave at a baseball game: First there is the single department or unit, then others follow.

To try open-book techniques in your own company, start with some of the ideas offered here, and then get a go-ahead to share a little more information. The more open your company, the better performance you're likely to see. And there is nothing like improved performance to quell people's fears of the unknown.

For Further Reading

The Great Game of Business by Jack Stack with Bo Burlingham (1994, Doubleday)

"Open-Book Management: Bulletin" (monthly newsletter edited by John Case)

Open-Book Management: The Coming Business Revolution by John Case (1995, HarperBusiness)

"Opening the Books" by John Case (*Harvard Business Review*, March–April 1997)

The Power of Open-Book Management by John P. Schuster, Jill Carpenter, with M. Patricia Kane (1996, John Wiley & Sons)

Reprint U9712A

Debriefing
Gabriel Szulanski

Improving Best-Practice Transfer

• • •

Lauren Keller Johnson

It all sounds so easy: The people in Unit A of your company are remarkably talented at, say, product design—and you want to duplicate their talent in Units B, C, and D. But when you try to transfer this best practice, the effort falls flat. Employees in Unit B prove unable to apply the practice. Those in Unit C balk at adopting it. And although workers in Unit D gamely implement the practice, the business results pale next to those of Unit A. Frustrated, you abandon the effort.

If it's any comfort, you're not alone. According to Gabriel Szulanski, author of *Sticky Knowledge: Barriers to Knowing in the Firm* and associate professor of strategy and management at INSEAD, most firms encounter huge difficulties in trying to spread best practices. And this is despite the abundance of "stellar performance in their own backyards." Unable to leverage existing knowledge, firms end up with performance gaps of 200% or more between comparable units—gaps worth millions.

How can executives make their companies' existing knowledge less "sticky" and capture the financial gains awaiting them if they can close those performance gaps? Szulanski says firms must recognize that there are unique challenges present in managing the transfer of internal knowledge, and so managers must look beyond familiar motivational factors—e.g., "source" employees' unwillingness to share data for fear of losing their jobs, or "recipient" employees' resistance to change. Managers, he says, must also attend to these seven *knowledge barriers*, which he breaks into four categories:

Knowledge characteristics

1. CAUSAL AMBIGUITY: We can't know with full certainty what's causing exceptional performance and how those forces might interact in another unit.

2. UNPROVEN KNOWLEDGE: When trying to transfer a recently developed best practice, we can't trust that knowledge to be effective in a new situation.

Source characteristics

3. LACK OF CREDIBILITY: High-performing unit members aren't perceived as knowledgeable or trustworthy by others in the organization.

Recipient characteristics

4. LACK OF ABSORPTIVE CAPACITY: People don't recognize the value of new knowledge. Moreover, they lack the skills, shared language, and experience to put new knowledge to work.

5. LACK OF RETENTIVE CAPACITY: People don't use transferred knowledge enough to embed it in the way they do their work.

Cultural characteristics

6. "BARRENNESS": The company lacks systems and structures to enable people to recognize and seize opportunities to leverage existing knowledge.

7. LACK OF "INTIMATE" RELATIONSHIPS BETWEEN SOURCES AND RECIPIENTS: People from different units don't have a history of positive communication and collaboration.

"Unsticking" Knowledge

According to Szulanski's research, the three most daunting knowledge barriers are causal ambiguity, recipient employees' lack of absorptive capacity, and lack of intimate relationships between sources and recipients.

Though we can't clear up causal ambiguity entirely, Szulanski says we *can* dig more deeply to discover why a successful practice works so well. "In companies where exemplary processes have been in place for 20 years," he says, "you need to ask people *why* they do what they do—and *how*. Consider your depth of knowledge of the practice, then ask yourself, 'What's the potential gain of applying this practice in another unit? How long will it take to start getting equal or better results in the recipient unit?' All knowledge barriers take time to remove, so you have to make a tradeoff."

Surmounting the absorptive-capacity barrier seems more straightforward. Indeed, Szulanski has seen many companies make a concerted effort to address this "stickiness predictor." Key strategies include investing in training and education to ensure that members of a recipient unit have the skills, along with the technical and managerial competence, to absorb the new practice. In addition, managers need to communicate the vision of what the company is trying to achieve through the transfer of existing knowledge. Finally, to improve their absorptive capacity, recipients must possess the vocabulary to talk about the transferred practice and must clearly define the roles and responsibilities essential for implementing the practice. If training and education don't yield results, Szulanski says, "managers should hire new people who *can* absorb the transferred practice."

As for the lack of intimate relationships between sources and recipients, Szulanski recommends doing whatever it takes to forge bonds between people. "In intimate relationships," he says, "people feel invested in those bonds. They enjoy interacting, they collaborate quickly and more productively, and they're more responsive to each other. All this is essential in best-practice transfer—because the two parties must interact repeatedly over long periods of time."

To foster close relationships, you can relax limits on travel and communication, and look for chances to promote teamwork between affected groups. "When Hewlett-Packard needed to transfer design practices from the U.S. to Singapore," Szulanski says, "it gave the two groups of engineers opportunities to spend time together under some fairly adverse circumstances. They went on treks [in] the Rocky Mountains—but the most powerful relationship-building experience they had involved eating Mexican food together. When you and your soon-to-be teammates are suffering from hot peppers, you bond pretty quickly!"

The Importance of Timing

Szulanski also advises managers to distinguish among four stages of best-practice transfer:

1. INITIATION: Recognizing and acting on an opportunity to transfer knowledge.

2. IMPLEMENTATION: Exchanging information and resources between source and recipient.

3. RAMP-UP: Beginning to use the transferred knowledge and rectifying unexpected problems.

4. INTEGRATION: Making the transferred practice routine.

"Different knowledge barriers become more of a problem at different stages," Szulanski says. For example, "Source credibility, proven-ness of knowledge, and causal ambiguity are particularly important during the initiation stage, whereas absorptive capacity becomes more of an issue during implementation, ramp-up, and integration." Equally important, "The sooner you start addressing knowledge barriers, the better—because they all take time to remove. If you wait too long to deal with them, you may already be up to your neck in costly mistakes."

Szulanski's study also explored the impact of motivational barriers at each of the four transfer stages. His findings revealed some surprising complexities. Specifically, it turns out that a recipient who's highly motivated to implement a best practice from another unit can actually *intensify* transfer problems during the ramp-up stage. Why? The person may prematurely dismiss outside help, expand seemingly straightforward modifications into major projects, make unnecessary changes to preserve pride of ownership and status, or switch to new practices at the worst possible moment because of unchecked enthusiasm. Recipients' motivation, Szulanski writes, "may therefore be helpful for initiating a transfer but may complicate its implementation."

To Copy or Not to Copy?

Szulanski's findings suggests several significant implications for managers. For one thing, "Managing for use of existing knowledge is different from managing to create *new* knowledge," he states. "In the first case, you want people to copy what's working well, get results, and only then start tinkering with the process to fix problems. In the second case, you'd probably want to *prohibit* copying. These are contradictory principles, so you have to be clear about when you're doing which."

In the face of causal ambiguity, "we must also accept that we don't know what we're doing—even while needing to act to keep our companies competitive. We have to be both humble and realistic—yet most of us have more confidence than we should in our ability to transfer knowledge." This makes copying even more important. As Szulanski explains, "If early on you start modifying a best practice you're trying to transfer, and then the effort fails in the new situation, you'll be even less able to determine *why* it failed. Your best hope of figuring out the cause of problems is to reproduce the source practice, then compare its new incarnation to the original. In a sense, you're trying to design as controlled an experiment as possible."

Last, Szulanski recommends identifying "a working example of the entire thing you want to copy. Don't cobble together 'the best of the best' or pieces of practices from different sources. A complete working example gives you your best shot at addressing most of the knowledge barriers. You see how the parts connect and interact, so right there, you're reducing causal ambiguity."

Szulanski's study suggests that obstacles to best-practice transfer are far more nuanced and complex than many of us realize. But by understanding the impact of knowledge as well as motivational barriers, we can improve our chances of transplanting exemplary performance across our organizations and better manage our companies' most precious source of competitive advantage.

Reprint U0403E

Are Your Employees Invested in the Bottom Line?

• • •

Traditional management thinking's emphasis on managing people "leads companies to spend billions of dollars on implementing management flavors of the month—producing what?" ask Jack Stack and coauthor Bo Burlingham in their recent book, *A Stake in the Outcome*. "A lot of cynicism and resistance to change," they answer.

But there is an alternative—one in which management helps people understand that they have a direct role in creating the kind of company they want. In such a system, write Stack and Burlingham, employees become so invested in hitting the company's financial targets that they take personal responsibility for individual budget lines in the income statement. In effect, their alignment with the company's goals enables them to manage themselves. Talk about a timely idea.

Stack, who pioneered the concept of open-book management, is president and CEO of Springfield Remanufacturing Corporation, an employee-owned company that supplies remanufactured engines to major automotive companies. In an interview with *Harvard Management Update,* he highlighted some of the ingredients that constitute such a culture.

Name a company that, in your estimation, has a culture of ownership.

Look at Southwest Airlines. In the weeks after the September 11 terrorist attacks, Southwest employees came up with cost-saving ideas, donated profit-sharing money, and signed over federal tax refund checks to the airline. But at other airlines, there was outrage as companies laid off thousands of workers, said they couldn't afford severance pay, and then asked the government for billions in emergency aid. Today, Southwest's total equity value is roughly $9 billion, whereas the total equity value of all the other airlines put together is around $7.5 billion.

What sets Southwest apart? Its employees feel like the airline is theirs.

Southwest employees own about 10% of the company. But United Airlines, which is about 55% employee-owned, is on the verge of bankruptcy. What do you make of that?

Equity in and of itself is not enough to create a culture of ownership. Of course, part of the problem is that we've cheapened the value of equity. Companies have used equity as a recruitment tool, but 85% of all the options that were given in *Fortune* 500 companies over the past 10 years didn't transfer into any kind of equity on the part of the employees. What's more, ownership has become an entitlement program. Companies have lent executives money to buy stock, and then they've forgiven the loans when the executives couldn't pay them back. This has created an instant-gratification mentality. Because they haven't sweated to earn the equity, many executives don't have what I call a psychic ownership mentality—they appreciate neither the value of ownership nor the responsibilities that come with it.

With psychic ownership, an employee almost doesn't need to be managed—because she's self-managed. In an ownership culture, every single budget line is owned by somebody inside the company. Everybody understands what their contribution to the company's overall performance is. Employees realize that, together, *they* make up the community that is the business, and *they* are the ones who set the company's standards and values—not just the guy in the corner office writing mission and vision statements. They carry out their functions not just so that they can get a merit increase at the end of the year, but because they're trying to build something for the long term.

Psychic ownership, then, seems to require something in addition to equity.

You want to have employees looking holistically at the business—how all the parts, such as R&D, marketing, customer service, and finance, fit together—the same way that a business takes an integrated view of its individual products and services.

Everything is so departmentalized today. If you're selling copiers, your performance objectives probably specify things like how many total calls you need to make each week, how many new calls you need to make, and how many plant tours you need to arrange. But there's nothing in that list of objectives that correlates with the company's overall sales plan. Wouldn't you think that part of the salesperson's job would be to help make the sales line of the company's income statement? Most companies don't even put it as part of the salesperson's accountability.

Companies are also too compartmentalized. They ask people to make a great product or provide a great service, but very few organizations ask their people to create a great company. They don't ask their employees to think outside their current roles or functions—to help figure out how to build the success of the overall entity. They don't capture that higher level of employees' intelligence.

Listening to the Ratios

Each year, Springfield Remanufacturing Corporation focuses on the two financial ratios that are most out of line relative to the industry standard. How does it use the ratios to align employee behavior? Let's say that *accounts receivable turnover* (total credit sales divided by the accounts receivable) is one of the ratios chosen. This ratio gives you an indication of how long it takes to collect your accounts receivable. "Most people assume that managing the accounts receivable is the finance department's responsibility," says President and CEO Jack Stack. But if the order you ship gets rejected by the customer's inspection department because you didn't send the right number of products, your payment will be delayed until the problem is resolved. "This is how things like poor employee morale or poor processes can create a situation where it takes your company three or four times as long as the industry average to collect its receivables," says Stack. "If you're a small company, that could affect your ability to make payroll. But most companies never

What's the role of business literacy education in all this?

We have a tremendous economic literacy problem here in the United States. It's the most amazing thing: people are going to work every single day, they're paying mortgages,

---

tell people like the guy who put the wrong number of pieces in the box that he has an impact on payroll.

"Reducing the accounts receivable turnover enables you to drive down your debt, which gives you a higher net income. The money you save on interest expense also boosts your profit. So to get everyone focused on improving the accounts receivable turnover, we'd take a portion of the improved cash flow that resulted from our efforts and put it in a special employees' bonus program. That makes it very obvious to people how they can make a difference.

"Over the long term, encourage employees to think in terms of the *price-to-earnings* ratio. What changes can you make to boost the P/E multiple? Imagine that an investor is thinking about buying your company—you want to take away all his reasons for not buying. Where would somebody find fault with your business? Is it in morale or quality? Are all your accounts receivable from one industry segment? Maybe your health care costs are out of line. Encourage employees to look at these indicators the way an outsider would."

---

they're using credit cards, they're saving for tuition and retirement—yet very few of them could answer the question "Is the company healthy?" And it's not only the employees' fault—most companies don't make that information understandable and accessible.

If people don't recognize the opportunity they have to create some financial security for themselves and for one another, they won't be motivated by it. That's why, for over 25 years, our company has been teaching employees the language of business—not only so they can understand what a 401(k) is, but also so they can understand what earnings multiples and margins are. As a result, our employees are in a better position to make the necessary investments of time and money that will create a safe future for themselves and their families.

Do you do anything special to encourage managers to think in terms of building the success of the overall entity?

I don't pick managers primarily based on skill levels— whether they understand machinery or are great information processors or fabulous buyers. My middle managers and front-line supervisors have to be able to understand and interpret financial ratios that come off balance sheets, income statements, and cash flow statements. Those ratios are always sending you a message about what you've got to fix in order to enhance value.

You also have to open up your books—show people how they fit into the big picture. Every week, our staff meeting consists of a conversation about the income statement and cash flow of the company and its subsidiaries. It's through this process of repetition that people grow to understand how to make a profit and what they have to do in order to be competitive. That understanding gives them confidence to be able to believe that they can attain their objectives.

For Further Reading

A Stake in the Outcome: Building a Culture of Ownership for the Long-Term Success of Your Business by Jack Stack and Bo Burlingham (2002, Doubleday Currency)

Reprint U0210B

Retaining Your Top Performers

. . .

You've got motivated employees—so what will you do to keep them? As the war for talent rages on, you need to design strategies for retaining your most valuable people. How to secure their loyalty to you, your department, and your company? Recognize that people are loyal to their groups—and encourage collaboration and cooperation to strengthen those groups. Watch for and address early signs of discontent. Use "stay interviews" to find out what people want to do next. Hire for retention—selecting people who embody your company's values. And help them see the purpose and importance of what they do.

Time to Get Serious About Talent Management

• • •

Kristen B. Donahue

Three alarming findings from recent McKinsey & Company studies of 13,000 senior managers in large and mid-size companies:

A mere 3% strongly agreed that their companies did a good job of developing people effectively.

Only 3% strongly agreed that their companies were effective at dealing with poor performers.

A meager 16% strongly agreed that their companies could even identify the high- and low-performing leaders.

This news hardly inspires confidence that the layoffs occurring right now are being handled in a way that improves corporate performance. Nor does it bode well for the future, because the structural forces that have given rise to the war for talent will remain in place for at least the next 20 years. For instance, the principal talent pool for leaders—workers under age 45—will shrink by 6% over the next decade. And job mobility is showing no signs of slowing down. Still, most firms continue to take what Laurence Prusak, executive director of the IBM Institute for Knowledge Management and coauthor of *In Good Company,* calls "a stealth approach" to talent management.

> The more tightly you squeeze resources, the more creative employees will be—at acquiring resources.

"Great talent management is not something that you delegate to the HR department," says Helen Handfield-Jones, Toronto-based senior practice consultant for McKinsey & Company and one of the authors of the upcoming book *The War for Talent*. "Senior leaders need to make it an integral part of their job."

Segment the Different Performance Levels in Your Talent Pool

"It really isn't helpful to look at overall attrition and retention rates," says Handfield-Jones. Focus on the retention rate of your best people and the attrition rate of your low performers. "The name of the game is to keep your best people as long as you can. Low performers need to be managed just as aggressively—but in the opposite direction. C players attract other C players. They're not good role models, they're not good coaches, they're not good mentors. The action can range from placing them in a different role, where they can perform better, to taking them out of the company entirely."

Invest in Social Capital

"Investments to enhance collaboration and cooperation are the *sine qua non* for talent expressing itself," says Prusak. "People stay in organizations because they are loyal to their buddies. They are not loyal to the firm. Those contracts were broken a long time ago. They are loyal to their groups. So make the groups stronger." And it is possible to develop trust, he adds—even in this day and age. "If there's a high level of trust in the organization, you're more likely to retain talented people because they feel more comfortable taking chances, which is how talent manages itself."

Differentiate the Free Agents from the Loyalists

The business media gives you the impression that everybody is a free agent—a worker who feels no ties to the organization and who jumps from project to project as often as the mood strikes. But in fact there's a large number of people for whom loyalty, community building, and being part of something bigger than themselves matter a great deal. "I think most organizations would be better off if they constructed HR systems and management approaches that dealt with both types," says Thomas H. Davenport, director of Accenture's Institute for Strategic Change in Boston and coauthor of *The Attention Economy*. "We need at least a two-hump camel, a bimodal distribution" that acknowledges the preferences of the loyalists as well as the free agents. If layoffs become necessary, he continues, start by laying off the people for whom the organizational affiliation is less important—the free agents.

Don't Forget the Hands and Heart

Talent management isn't simply a matter of paying attention to the *head*, Teresa M. Amabile's metaphor for expertise. The Edsel Bryant Ford Professor of Business Administration at Harvard Business School, Amabile says you also have to consider the *hands* (the ability to take what you know and shape it into something that is "appropriately novel") and the *heart* (passion, a person's intrinsic motivation). "Organizations need to provide a cultural environment that encourages these three components that are essential for creativity." Specifically:

- Make sure employees are carefully matched to the work they are doing. Place them "at an optimal challenge level," advises Amabile, "the top of their skill level where they are going to continue to develop their skills."

- Give them freedom—"some sense of control over their own work" and also the time to pursue their ideas

- Provide adequate resources. "It is true that the more tightly you squeeze resources, the more creative people will be, but they will be creative at getting resources—they won't necessarily be creative at doing the real important work you want them to do."

- Make sure you're sending the right signals. "If you only promote people who follow the rules," says Prusak, "you don't get wild ducks" [IBM's term for eccentric but highly creative employees].

Social Networks—Or Social Darwinism?

Nothing beats a passionate debate. Here's a blow-by-blow account taken from a recent panel discussion sponsored by Harvard Business School Publishing about the merits of a meritocratic approach to managing your top-level managers. Helen Handfield-Jones, senior practice consultant with McKinsey & Company; Laurence (Larry) Prusak, executive director of the IBM Institute for Knowledge Management; and Teresa M. Amabile, professor of business administration at Harvard Business School, all weighed in on the topic.

Handfield-Jones: Take the top-level managers in any company: there are the 20% that are the best; there's a whole bunch in the middle; and there are some 20% at the bottom who are contributing the least. Companies need to be much more aggressive about looking at the bottom of their talent pool and taking action. That action can range from putting those people into roles where they can succeed to asking them to leave the company. This is important not just because of the performance differential, but also because of the impact it has on the rest of the talent pool. Eighty percent of the managers in our survey who had worked for a low-performing boss at one time in their career said it made them want to leave the company—it prevented them from learning and from making a bigger contribution.

Prusak: That takes a totally apolitical view of organizations. You're positing a total meritocracy, which I have never seen in any organization. People protect each other. People work with each other. UPS, for example, is a very successful firm. They have very low turnover. They'll be a very successful firm 100 years from now because they really care about people and they don't make these Darwinian judgments on low or high performance. IBM has 340,000 people. I assure you we have Nobel Prize winners and Beavis and Butthead—a natural distribution of talent. Who makes the call of who's Beavis and who's Einstein? Moreover, are you going to chop off 20% of the workforce at the end of every two years and replace them? It would cost you a fortune; it would wreck morale; it would wreck communities and work teams. It just wouldn't work in large, process-based organizations.

Amabile: When I first heard Helen's views, my reaction was the same as Larry's. On the other hand, I did a study of 26 creative teams in different organizations. I gave them an electronic diary and asked them to send entries

(continued)

(continued)

back to me every day. Out of those 26 teams, it was clear in three or four cases that the manager of the team was destroying it. We found an outsize impact of management at any level—simple things can make a huge difference. So you have to be very careful about who you put into management roles, and be prepared to rotate people out of those roles if things don't seem to be working.

Handfield-Jones: We asked the managers in our survey, "Would you be delighted if your company more aggressively moved on low performers, either out of the organization or out of critical leadership positions?" Fifty-eight percent strongly agreed, and 96% strongly or somewhat agreed. It's a critical responsibility of the leaders of a company to get good at assessing the managerial talent pool. To not do it at all because you say it will be flawed is wrong. It will never be perfect, but you can get it fairly robust. Organizations that keep the standards high for leaders are more high-performing and more energized, not less so.

Talent management can sometimes seem just as mysterious as human beings are at their core. Then again, some of those mysteries might reveal themselves if companies researched the topic as assiduously as they did, say, marketing during the 1960s and 1970s. If companies are serious when they say that people represent their most valuable asset, then it's high time for them to start managing that asset more aggressively—and more thoughtfully.

For Further Reading

In Good Company: How Social Capital Makes Organizations Work by Don Cohen and Laurence Prusak (2001, Harvard Business School Press)

The War for Talent by Helen Handfield-Jones, Ed Michaels, and Beth Axelrod (2001, Harvard Business School Press)

"How to Kill Creativity" by Teresa M. Amabile (*Harvard Business Review,* September–October 1998)

"Knowledge Management: Beyond Databases" by Kristen B. Donahue (*Harvard Management Update,* May 2001)

"The War for Managerial Talent" (*Harvard Management Update,* March 2001)

"A New Retention Strategy: Focusing on Individuals" (*Harvard Management Update,* January 2001)

Reprint U0107C

A New Retention Strategy

Focusing on Individuals

•   •   •

"Happy families are all alike," begins Tolstoy's famous introduction to *Anna Karenina*. But happy employees aren't alike at all. One really values his company's generous wages and benefits. Another feels underpaid yet appreciates the career opportunities afforded by her company's rapid growth. A third thrives on his employer's fiercely competitive culture.

This observation—people really are different—is hard to dispute, but policies aimed at reducing employee turnover often ignore it. Companies raise salaries for whole categories of people without considering how many individuals stay mostly for the money. They announce costly perks such as tuition reimbursement without knowing whether employees might prefer something else. They use the same retention techniques for salespeople, say, as for computer programmers—even though the two groups are likely to have very different interests.

Big, across-the-board programs have an obvious logic. They fit the standard operating procedures of a bureaucracy and allow managers to avoid charges of favoritism. But with high turnover rates a perennial and seemingly intractable problem these days, companies may need a more tailored approach. "You have to look at what individuals want," said Charlotte Evans, VP of HR at the consulting firm Linkage Inc., to a recent conference of the Northeast Human Resources Association. One reason: according to a research report from Linkage, a high-performing employee is worth five times more to a company than a lower performer.

Cast a wide net—create tailored opportunities for individuals at all levels whom your company wants to keep.

Of course, no company should treat individuals so differently that it runs afoul of antidiscrimination rules and other labor laws. But within those constraints, say HR specialists, there's a lot of latitude for customized retention strategies.

1: Hire for Retention

This means looking beyond skills and experience to individual values and attitudes. Retention always begins with recruitment, say the experts, and one key is to avoid bringing in employees who are guaranteed to be unhappy. "Hire people who fit what you value," urges Andy Esparza, VP of global staffing for Dell Computer Corp. Among the traits Dell looks for in an employee are the ability to deal with ambiguity and what the company delicately calls "organizational agility." Example: a recruit may find that her job has changed before she even shows up for her first day at work. People who value stability and predictability would be a poor match.

Another key to hiring for retention: give people a thorough and accurate description—warts and all—of the company and job they're applying for. The temptation, given the tight labor market and the war for the most talented people, is to soft-pedal the less appealing elements. But such a tactic proves short-sighted when you consider the costs of turnover. Troy State University Florida Region professors Maureen Hannay and Melissa

Northam conducted a survey of nearly 200 working adults and found that bridging the "expectations gap" is one of the cheapest and most effective retention tactics an employer can pursue. "Our findings clearly show that simply providing employees with realistic job previews, in which they are informed of both the positive and negative aspects of the job, can reduce turnover," they report in the journal *Compensation and Benefits Review.*

2: Research What Particular Groups of Employees Want

Identify the "root causes" of turnover among specific groups of employees, advises a recent study by Sibson & Company, a consulting firm with offices in New York City

The "Stay" Interview

Everybody does exit interviews, says Michael Cassani, but how many companies talk to their employees month in and month out about how they're enjoying their jobs, what they'd like to do next, and so on? Cassani, director of employment and employee relations at Private Healthcare Systems counsels line managers to conduct such interviews regularly and to keep an ear out for early signs of discontent, such as unexplained absences. "You have to start talking to people before they leave, not just when they leave," he says.

and elsewhere. Sibson's research, for example, showed that the single most important variable in retaining stockbrokers is generous financial incentives. Other approaches—programs emphasizing career development, for example—are "just not worth the investment."

Following this precept, a health-services company found that its call-center employees wanted a chance to advance without leaving the call center, and that they would welcome the opportunity to learn the jobs of colleagues who dealt with different groups of clients. When the company instituted four grade levels and a job-swapping program, turnover declined. Charles Schwab, the big financial-services firm, conducts regular employee surveys about job satisfaction. But rather than simply compile results at the company level, Schwab "narrows the replies to individual departments and holds front-line managers responsible for addressing any serious problems that surface," reports *Training* magazine.

3: Structure the Company to Allow Choices

Some employees want more money, others more time off. Some need health insurance and retirement plans; others don't. So-called cafeteria benefit plans are making headway, but many companies persist in one-size-fits-all programs, or programs that target one group while ignoring others. It's great to provide subsidized day care for parents of young children, for example—but is there a corresponding benefit for employees who don't have kids? In one imaginative variation on the cafeteria-plan concept, FleetBoston Financial allows some employees to buy and sell a certain number of vacation days, thereby providing employees with different preferences the abil ity to swap cash for leisure or vice versa.

Another form of choice that can be important to employees is different career paths. Nearly every company includes people who want to advance in a particular functional or professional area (sales, engineering, design, etc.) and others who hope to advance through the managerial ranks. The two groups have different career goals, different ways of measuring their success, and different preferences about how they spend their time, points out Cliff Balzer, a manager of organizational development for Shaw's Supermarkets, in a recent issue of *Insights* magazine. Yet many companies take their most successful specialists and make them managers— and people go along with it because that's their only avenue to promotion and a higher salary.

4: Single Out People for Special Programs

Organizations profess to be nervous about offering special opportunities to individuals, but of course they do it all the time. Some people are fast-tracked while others languish. Some are promoted or given raises, others aren't. From a retention perspective, the trick is to cast a wide net—and to create tailored opportunities for individuals at all levels whom the company wants to keep. Does someone want a brief (unpaid) leave of absence? Tuition support for a class that doesn't fit the guidelines? One company offers internal internships to employees who want to learn a different department's work; the interns often fill in for new mothers who are out on three-month maternity leaves. Fleet's human resources department sponsors a so-called Best in Class program, which provides high-performing HR employees with special assignments that broaden their experience and deepen their skills. Of the 29 program graduates in the three years since the program began, reports Fleet's Billie Jean Potter, only four have left the bank.

"Companies must find a way to know who their best are, figure out what those employees want and need, make sure that they are getting it, and make sure that they know that they're getting it," writes Phil Harkins, president and CEO of Linkage, in his introduction to the firm's recent report *The Brave New World of Recruiting and Retention.* "The old rules of treating everyone the same are for the Old Economy."

For Further Reading

Finding & Keeping Great Employees by Jim Harris, Ph.D. and Joan Brannick, Ph.D. (1999, AMACOM Books)

Keeping the People Who Keep You in Business: 24 Ways to Hang on to Your Most Valuable Talent by Leigh Branham (2001, AMACOM Books)

Love 'Em or Lose 'Em: Getting Good People to Stay by Beverly Kaye and Sharon Jordan-Evans (1999, Berrett-Koehler Publishers)

Reprint U0101A

Nine Steps
Toward Creating
a Great Workplace

· · ·

Creating a great workplace isn't all a matter of perks, says Robert Levering of the Great Place to Work Institute in San Francisco, which compiles the *Fortune* list of the 100 best companies to work for in America. Rather, a great workplace is one where people are engaged in their jobs, where there's mutual respect between employees and management, and where people feel that they're treated fairly. Benefits are important, he adds, but they're a reflection of the underlying culture, not the cause of it. What's more, the best workplaces *get* as much as they *give*. Consulting firm Kepner-Tregoe, recently completed an in-depth study of several "retention leaders"—companies with low employee turnover rates. The study found that these firms balanced high performance standards with a near-obsessive regard for their employees' well-being.

And the real news about creating a great workplace is this: as a manager, you don't need to stand on the sidelines waiting for big, centralized, companywide programs. The Gallup Organization interviewed about one million workers (including 80,000 managers) over the last 25 years, asking them about all aspects of their work life. It found that even in the best companies, retention, productivity, and worker satisfaction all vary greatly from unit to unit. "People may join a company because of its brand identity," explains Gallup senior VP Marcus Buckingham, "but how long they stay depends to a great extent on the quality of their manager."

To some managers, this isn't surprising. "I've talked with many employees who stay in a work situation because they like their supervisor so much," notes David Pulatie, a senior VP at Motorola. "When people see their manager going out of the way for them, that's an enormous attraction."

How can you start creating a great workplace right here, right now, in your unit?

1: Help People See the Purpose of What They Do

According to Kepner-Tregoe CEO Quinn Spitzer, people stay at jobs that are intellectually stimulating or personally rewarding. Unfortunately, many jobs seem to have neither attribute. "That's why Dilbert is so popular," says Spitzer. "He strikes a resonant chord about the fundamental drudgery of work." But even repetitive jobs can be infused with meaning if employees understand how what they do drives the company's objectives and contributes to business success. "Take someone who packages and sterilizes medical products," says Tom Rochon, a VP of human resources with Ethicon Endo Surgery, in Cincinnati. "We help them understand the importance [to the company] of putting products to market in a certain amount of time and with a certain quality."

If your people do many different things—writing reports, talking to customers, attending meetings, and so on—ask them to rank these tasks by how important they think each one is to the organization. What you hear may surprise you. "I talked with an employee in one of the 'best' companies," recalls Spitzer. "She said she would be willing to commit to anything as long as she didn't have to go to another meeting. She saw these meetings as a callous disregard for her time." If you hear such responses and you think people are wrong in their perceptions—if those meetings really are important—help them understand why and how all those "unimportant" tasks matter.

2: Expect a Lot

Challenge people not only to meet their goals but to exceed them, advises Keric DeChant, VP of strategic sales development at Stryker Corp., a maker of medical equipment. When DeChant was midwest sales manager, he made it clear to his sales reps that he expected them to perform as a team even though they were paid straight commission—and to hit group goals, not just their own. One rep, he recalls, met his yearly sales target by October and could have coasted for the rest of the year. Instead he raised his team's numbers by continuing to sell, and in fact had his biggest month in December. "I never had to ask my reps for numbers," says DeChant. "They just knew my expectations of them, and they eventually had the same expectations of themselves and of the team."

3: But Don't Dictate the "How"

Nature tells us that the best route from A to B isn't always a straight line, it's the path of least resistance. So while good companies set high standards, they're flexible about how they let people meet those standards. One salesperson might sell through relationship building, another through sheer technical competence, a third by calling more prospects. If they're all top sellers, does it matter how they got there? "If you standardize the end," says Gallup's Buckingham, "you don't have to standardize the means."

4: Be *Really* Available

Levering found that managers' availability was a crucial variable in the companies he surveyed for *Fortune*. "Most of us are distrustful in work situations because there's such a huge power imbalance," he notes. "That makes it extremely important to make management accessible." If you want to know how accessible you are, says Kepner-Tregoe's Spitzer, look at last year's appointment calendar. Try to identify how much time you spent talking to employees about their agendas. "If you're not spending 10% at it," he says, "you don't have a satisfied work force."

Availability may require a physical move. Bruce McLenitham, who manages Steelcase North America's chair plant, was the first plant manager in the company to move his office to the factory floor. Why? "I'm the factory manager, not the office manager," he quips. "You go where your customer is—and I look at every employee as a customer." The move enhanced both morale and productivity, he says, and other plant managers have since followed suit. McLenitham also makes a point of getting to know people on a personal level. "I know everyone's name," he says. "I know their kids' names and their dogs' names. I have an employee who plays hockey. The day after his games I make an effort to ask him how it went."

5: Break the Golden Rule

You may hate micromanagement, but some of your people may want to be checked in with every day. And just because you like to make decisions doesn't mean everyone does. "If you put someone like that in a role where they have to make decisions, you're creating lots of stress," says McLenitham. Instead, give the job to someone who thrives on decision making. Tasks can be tailored to the individual as well. "A couple of people might like paperwork. Some prefer working on computers—let them do the graphs." Treat people not as you would like to be treated, but as *they* would like to be treated.

6: Get the Word Out— in 24 Hours or Less

Bob Nelson was a department manager at Blanchard Training and Development in San Diego, with 16 people in his department. "I made a commitment that within 24 hours of any management meeting, I would meet with my department and discuss the implications of the meeting for their jobs." The result? "They felt treated like colleagues," says Nelson. "Another manager said,

How Good Is Your Workplace?

Job satisfaction is notoriously hard to measure—but a Gallup study of one million workers found that satisfaction depends on how employees answer just 12 questions, listed below in order of importance. To assess your workplace, ask people for their responses:

1. Do I know what is expected of me at work?
2. Do I have the materials and equipment I need to do my work right?
3. At work, do I have the opportunity to do what I do best every day?
4. In the last seven days, have I received recognition or praise for good work?
5. Does my supervisor or someone else at work seem to care about me as a person?
6. Is there someone at work who encourages my development?
7. At work, do my opinions seem to count?
8. Does the mission of my company make me feel like my work is important?
9. Are my coworkers committed to doing quality work?
10. Do I have a best friend at work?
11. In the last six months, have I talked with someone about my progress?
12. At work, have I had opportunities to learn and grow?

'Your people are so pumped up about what you're doing—how do you do it?'"

7: Make Sure People Have What They Need to Do Their Jobs

The Gallup study found that, next to knowing what was expected of them, what made employees most productive was being given the materials and equipment they needed for their jobs. The implications? "If an employee needs a software upgrade to do her job effectively," says Nelson, "then go to bat with the company to help her get it."

8: Say Thanks

Great workplaces put a lot of time and energy into making people feel special. That's the real value of perks like in-house manicures. But appreciation doesn't have to cost a lot of money. Rochon's company, for example, encourages supervisors to recognize employees (and employees to recognize each other) for a job well done. If a team spends a weekend wrapping up a project, each person might get a video coupon, $5 for the cafeteria, or a pizza. "The key is speed," he says. "The reward has to be given on the spot." And though the rewards are small, they go a long way. "A lot of people tell us, 'You don't know how much it meant.'"

9: Have Fun!

McLenitham throws a picnic when his plant meets its safety numbers. The managers do the cooking. On employees' birthdays, supervisors give the employee a sheet telling them what happened on that day in history. "It's not much, but it helps build a relationship."

Sometimes, poking a little fun is the best way to make a serious point. McLenitham, for instance, does a "man on the street" video once a month. "We had trouble having people fill out scrap forms. So I had someone film me on a machine making parts. I got a bad part, got angry, and threw it in the trash. A coordinator came up and said, 'Hey, you can't throw that away without filling out the scrap form.' So I stomped into the plant manager's office screaming and yelling. A guy doing an impression of me told me how filling out the forms will give us data to reduce defects."

It must have been a great video. McLenitham says that the plant's scrap reporting has been excellent since he made it.

For Further Reading

"One More Time: How Do You Motivate Employees?" by Frederick Hertzberg (*Harvard Business Review*, September–October 1987)

Avoiding the Brain Drain: What Companies Are Doing to Lock in Their Talent (November 1998, Kepner-Tregoe, Inc.)

1001 Ways to Energize Employees by Bob Nelson (1997, Workman Publishing)

"The 100 Best Companies to Work for in America," by Shelly Branch (*Fortune,* January 11, 1999)

First, Break All the Rules: What the World's Greatest Managers Do Differently by Marcus Buckingham and Curt Coffman (1999, Simon & Schuster)

Reprint U9903A

Satisfaction

The False Path to Employee Loyalty

• • •

Frederick F. Reichheld

General Norman Schwarzkopf told me once how his lieutenants in Vietnam unintentionally destroyed the foundations of their soldiers' loyalty. When the troopers complained about wearing hot, bulky flak jackets in the steamy jungle, he said, the lieutenants tried to build loyalty by being nice and made flak jackets optional. Later, when the squad came under attack, casualties skyrocketed. Afterward, Schwarzkopf made sure that the lesson was well understood: "Loyalty is not about putting the comfort of your people first; it is about putting their welfare first."

This was a critical lesson for the military—and it's critical in the business world, too. In good times, business leaders too often give undue attention to employee comfort, in the belief that employee satisfaction surveys hold the key to loyalty. This confusion of satisfaction with loyalty constitutes one of the greatest betrayals in the business world. The strongest businesses, it turns out those with the most loyal employees and customers—are the ones in which employees are frequently *dissatisfied*.

The point here is not to try to make your employees irritable. This isn't about serving them cheap coffee, or limiting access to free pens and such—it's about giving your organization an edge that will serve it well in this unforgiving, competitive economy. It's about making sure that employees are dissatisfied with the level of service they're able to provide customers, and as a result, motivated to reach a higher level. Real employee loyalty is generated when employees, unhappy with the status quo, are constantly reaching to deliver the kind of value and service that develops increasingly loyal customers.

In bad times, it's all too easy to separate those businesses with truly loyal employees and customers from those whose constituencies report that they are merely "satisfied." Leaders who have managed for employee satisfaction will most likely be forced to watch helplessly as their businesses are bushwacked by the competition. They'll have the most devastating layoffs. Their remaining employees will be injured as well: They'll strain under heavier workloads as they take up the slack from departing employees. Their pride and motivation will suffer as customers defect to competitors who offer superior value. And their trust in the company's leadership will erode as career growth opportunities diminish.

> At least half the teams in American companies are too large to foster superior loyalty.

How can you ensure that you're managing for your employees' welfare rather than their satisfaction? Here are two key pieces of the puzzle:

- Structure your organization into the right teams to foster responsiveness and accountability.

- Provide those teams with the tools they need to monitor how well they're creating the kind of value necessary to earn customer loyalty.

For the second dimension, the Loyalty Acid Test, a survey of employees and customers created by Bain & Company, can help companies monitor their efforts to build loyalty. The average firm, we've found, is lucky if half its employees agree that their employer is worthy of loyalty. Although 75% of customers say they are satisfied or very satisfied, our research indicates that only 50% to 55% are actually loyal—which is really no surprise if only half the employees with whom they interact believe their firm is worthy of loyalty.

Now for the hard part: leaders must ensure that team structures facilitate loyalty. Consider, again, the military. Patriotic emotions, trust in leadership, belief in the principles of the Constitution, a desire to make the world a safer and better place—all these elements strengthen the bonds of loyalty. But the military has learned that the essential management device that makes those beliefs and desires practical and operational is the small team in which individual soldiers operate. Small units, made up of 5-10 soldiers, provide clear visibility and accountability. Everyone's role is vital because there is no slack, and even in chaotic battle conditions, rapid communication and coordination are still possible.

The same holds true in business. The dynamics of small teams bond members to one another. If the organizational goal of serving customers isn't being met, there's no place to hide, no administrative machinery to fill in the gaps. If the goal is to be achieved, team members know it's up to them.

In the companies I call loyalty leaders, the average team size is far smaller than at the competition. At

USAA, call center teams have 10–12 members; its competitors' teams have 17–25. At Southwest Airlines there are 10 employees per supervisor—half the airline industry average. At Enterprise Rent-A-Car, the average team size is eight; competitors' teams are three times larger. These companies are not fooled by the accounting logic that small teams drive up costs ("All those expensive supervisors!"). Instead, they know that small teams, when properly utilized, result not only in the lowest costs in the industry, but also the highest levels of service.

Most executives think they know the benefits of small teams: 71% of the executives we surveyed reported that they keep organizational structure simple by utilizing small teams. But when we interviewed frontline employees, only 43% agreed that small teams were being effectively utilized. And when we asked them how many other employees report to the same individual, we discovered that small teams are not nearly as prevalent as one might think.

Business leaders are stacking the deck against themselves in their quest to earn superior loyalty by allowing their teams to grow to bloated dimensions. Bain's research reveals that at least half the teams in American companies are too large to foster superior loyalty. Small teams have the highest levels of employee loyalty; on average, a team of seven or fewer scores 15 percentage points higher on employee loyalty than teams of more than 25.

Avoiding Team Inflation

Most successful teams tend to increase in size unless leaders get personally involved in splitting them up. Andy Taylor, CEO of Enterprise Rent-A-Car, has implemented an ironclad rule that whenever one of his branches grows to a certain size—usually between 100 and 200 cars—that branch is divided in two. Branch managers understand that although it is not very motivating to give away half the employees they've hired and trained—and half the customer base they've built—the only way to get promoted is to grow a profitable branch that divides into multiple branches. They also know that they must deliver the kind of service that makes customers want to come back. Using its own abbreviated customer acid test, Enterprise surveys each one of its more than 4,500 branches monthly to determine customer satisfaction and intention to return. Only the managers in the branches with scores ranking in the top half are eligible for promotion. By keeping teams small, and by keeping them focused on customer experience in addition to profits and growth, senior management is helping ensure that Enterprise beats the competition.

At Chick-fil-A, the loyalty leader in quick-serve restaurants, chairman S. Truett Cathy has long insisted that a store manager should run just one store. He attributes much of the firm's success—most of his stores enjoy greater sales per square foot than the bigger chains—to the structural advantage of small, local teams. Even though the competition encourages successful operators to manage additional units, Cathy has fiercely resisted organizational pressure to do the same—until recently, that is, when a few of his operators convinced him that they could handle the challenge of running larger teams. Although Cathy relented, he also insisted that these operators monitor customer satisfaction carefully. Only the few managers who had superior customer satisfaction levels were allowed to keep their second store, and only as long as they continued to pass the monthly acid test with their customers.

Perks are nice; they can even help you attract and retain the talent you want most. But the source of genuine employee loyalty lies elsewhere. Employee loyalty and customer loyalty are closely linked: to reap the benefits of customer loyalty, you must first earn your employees' loyalty. So keep the size of your teams small, and give employees the tools they need to build strong relationships with customers.

Reprint U0110C

Selecting the Right Rewards, Recognition, and Incentives

• • •

None of us can honestly say that financial incentives don't matter in our professional lives. After all, we've got mortgages, college tuition, and other expenses to manage. But money alone isn't enough to motivate people to excel on the job. In fact, the most effective incentive systems blend monetary with nonmonetary forms of reward—and often it's the nonmonetary types that prove the most motivating. How to choose the right mix of rewards? Understand what employees most value: basic praise, the authority to do their work and make decisions, and support from their managers when they've made a mistake. In the compensation half of your incentives equation, consider letting employees select from a menu including cash, restricted shares, and options—and tying variable compensation to achievement of performance targets. You'll give your people a direct line of sight between their on-the-job accomplishments and the rewards they receive.

Employee Recognition and Reward with Bob Nelson

• • •

In this economic climate, it is more critical than ever to make your staff feel recognized for their contributions. The *Harvard Management Update* sought the advice of best-selling author and employee motivation expert Bob Nelson, who has worked with such companies as FedEx, Time Warner, and IBM, on how to best handle this.

1. What's so important about informal, manager-initiated recognition?

It's important because recognition is about feeling special, and more times than not, it is hard to feel special from a corporate program where everyone gets the same thing, like a five-year pin. To be effective, recognition needs to come from those we hold in high esteem, such as one's manager.

2. What is necessary for delivering effective informal recognition?

Timing is important. The sooner you acknowledge employees' performance, the clearer they get the message, the more likely they are to repeat the desired performance.

Recognition is most powerful when it's contingent. Companies will bring in doughnuts on Friday and give people cards on their birthday, and all of a sudden you've got an entitlement culture. If you do stuff just to be nice, people end up expecting more. So make recognition contingent upon desired behavior and performance; they'll value the recogntion more and you'll get better results.

And you have got to keep it fresh, relevant, and sincere. Any incentive has less punch with repeated use.

3. What kinds of recognition and rewards do employees want most?

I conducted an Internet survey that gave people choices of 52 items. The No. 1 factor they valued was "managerial support and involvement"—asking employees their opinions, involving them in decisions, giving them authority to do their jobs, supporting them when they make a mistake, and so forth. Also important were flexible working hours, learning and development opportunities, manager availability, and time.

Employees also want basic praise. In the top 10 factors, there were four types of praise: personal praise, written praise, public praise, and electronic praise. Those are the hottest ones for people, and none of them costs a dime!

4. How do you choose what type of praise to use in a given situation?

Weigh these factors:

* Availability of the medium: How often do you actually see the individual do you manage him from a distance or does he telecommute? Do you have occasion for public praise such as periodic staff meetings?

- Employee preference: Do you know how the employee prefers to be praised—have you ever discussed it with her? For example, an introverted employee would likely prefer a written or electronic note versus public recognition.

- Manager comfort zone: What forms of praise are you comfortable giving? If you feel awkward giving face-to-face praise, for example, you probably won't do it even if you feel you should. If you are uncomfortable speaking publicly, it might be better to skip public praise for something that is more personal and sincere.

5. Are there special considerations to delivering recognition in tough economic conditions?

Yes. The times when we need to do it the most, we tend to do it least. Say you give a team award that used to come with $250 but because you can't afford the $250, you stop giving the team award anymore. I say still give the team award. Say something like, "We've had to drop the financial aspect to hunker down, but it doesn't diminish the value of the job that this team did, especially at this time." When we are up against it, just a word of support, a team lunch, a "hang in there," can go a very long way.

For Further Reading

Make Their Day! Employee Recognition That Works by Cindy Ventrice (2003, Berrett-Koehler)

The Magic of Employee Recognition: 10 Proven Tactics from CalPERS and Disney by Dee Hansford (2003, Worldat-Work)

Other People's Habits: How to Use Positive Reinforcement to Bring Out the Best in People Around You by Aubrey C. Daniels (2000, McGraw-Hill)

Reprint U0309D

Rethinking Money and Motivation

...

Loren Gary

Ever heard the advice "Do what you love, and the money will follow?" The idea here is that concerns about money only confuse the search for what's intrinsically motivating. For at least the past half-century, leading management thinkers have supported such an understanding. Today, however, with money so central to all aspects of contemporary life, some are beginning to believe that candid conversations about money might clarify rather than cloud workers' search for their most deep-seated interests.

Giving compensation a more prominent place in discussions between managers and employees might seem to fly in the face of conventional wisdom. As Frederick Herzberg notes in his famous 1968 *Harvard Business Review* article, "One More Time: How Do You Motivate Employees?" money, perks, workplace conditions, and company policy and administration are all "hygiene factors"—extrinsic to the job itself. They aren't enough to generate employee commitment. For sustained performance improvement, Herzberg argues, only intrinsic motivators such as job enrichment, which responds to employees' abiding need for growth and achievement by making their work more challenging and interesting, will do the trick.

As American society has become more affluent, however, say many social critics and executive coaches, people seem to be working more than ever—but having increasing difficulty finding meaning and purpose in their lives. In previous generations, people had "lots of different sources of meaning and affirmation, including the neighborhood, civic activities, and religious organizations," says executive coach Pamela York Klainer. "Now, aside from raising their families, they mostly just work." So the workplace has become the primary arena in which people search for meaning. And the accumulation of money "has become the most tangible indicator that we're making progress in this search," she says.

"People have this unexamined belief that their income will always go up and that the company is disrespecting them if it doesn't give them an annual increase," says Klainer, author of *How Much Is Enough?* To help dispel this notion, managers can educate employees in a few basic principles of business finance, thereby removing much of the psychodrama from salary discussions and instead turning them into "rational conversations about the constraints on what the company can do for an employee given its financial performance in a particular year," she says.

For example, make sure direct reports understand the difference between the company's revenues and its profitability. Explain the way that markets define worth (as a combination of pricing and brand value). Show them how their work contributes to the company's bottom line. Out of this business literacy grows the understanding that the money may not always follow when we do what we love— we must often make tradeoffs between the two.

This realization can restore to us a sense of the limits of what money can provide, writes San Francisco State University philosophy professor Jacob Needleman in *Money and the Meaning of Life*. In a money-sodden culture, he says, "people easily confuse their fundamental material needs"—the striving to secure the food, clothing, shelter, and safety we need to survive—"with the equally fundamental spiritual needs for a sense of meaning and purpose in our lives." They have trouble distinguishing their intrinsic love for a certain kind of work from their desire to have all the comforts and protection that money can buy.

Paradoxically, it's only by paying more attention to money—especially the fears and self-deceptions that it occasions in our lives—that we can begin to recover an understanding of the differences between these two basic human needs. Taking money more seriously helps us move beyond our preoccupation with it, says Needleman. Only then can we see all the possibilities for achievement, meaning, and connection that exist beyond the quest for survival.

An unflinching look at our attitudes and beliefs about money can help us identify our intrinsic motivations and lead us to a richer understanding of the deep-seated sources of interest and fulfillment that money can never satisfy.

Reprint U0404F

Which Incentives Pay Off Now?

• • •

Peter Jacobs

Who could blame Microsoft for doing away with stock option grants? The corporate world has gotten an enormous black eye over gross excesses in the use of options, the Financial Accounting Standards Board appears poised to require firms to treat them as compensation expense, and a vigorous debate continues over their effectiveness in employee motivation. Plenty of companies would just as soon be done with options altogether.

But many others—Citigroup, for one—remain committed to using option grants at all organizational levels. In fact, Citigroup already expenses options in the compensation packages of tens of thousands of its

North American employees. It also gives those receiving stock-based compensation greater choice in the form of such pay—between options and restricted stock—while tightening the conditions under which options can be exercised.

But from the deliberations over the role of stock options at Microsoft and Citigroup and scores of other firms, a broader discussion has emerged on how to create a more meaningful connection between pay and corporate strategy. While many firms are still in the exploratory stages, others have already begun carving out new turf. Their approaches reflect fresh thinking about the way we motivate and remunerate everyone, from front-line workers to top executives, in the contemporary workplace.

The Options Beyond Options

Although the role of options is not the whole of the compensation discussion, it's certainly at the center of it. Mercer Management's Peter Chingos likens the environment to the weather phenomenon described in author Sebastian Junger's *The Perfect Storm.* "A lot of things are happening simultaneously," Chingos says. Companies are suddenly facing the need to expense options, the number of options they have outstanding and the potential for earnings dilution have become enormous, a major market decline has driven many options under water, and investors are irate over runaway CEO pay.

There's also the question of how effective a motivational tool options really are. For example, in "The Trouble with Stock Options," an article in the *Journal of Economic Perspectives,* Harvard Business School professor Brian Hall and University of Southern California professor Kevin Murphy look closely at the problems of using options in long-term incentive plans (LTIPs). Among such problems, they find, is the relatively weak ability of options to motivate employee performance during market downturns, and, conversely, the relatively large rewards they provide poor and mediocre performers during boom markets.

And the effects of the burgeoning case against an options-only equity approach? "Companies are seeking compensation vehicles that are based less on accounting methods and more on business objectives," says Gary Locke, who leads the executive compensation practice at consulting firm Towers Perrin.

Among the several trends Chingos notes is the shift toward greater diversification in LTIPs as some companies scale back the use of stock options and replace them with some combination of time- and performance-restricted shares of equivalent value. In addition, he says some firms are reallocating part of the present value of their LTIPs to the cash components of their compensation packages for midlevel management and below. This is prompted by the discovery that employees frequently exercise stock options as soon as practicable after vesting, effectively using them as cash compensation.

Another early trend, Chingos says, is the introduction of choice in LTIPs, so that executives can select from a menu that might include cash, restricted shares, and options.

Daring Directions

Companies considering their future compensation strategies should look at what others are doing:

Inverted Bonus Plan

At the heart of Planar Systems' approach to variable compensation is a commitment to senior executives. The commitment is to put them at the bottom of the pecking order.

Balaji Krishnamurthy, CEO of the publicly traded flat-panel display systems producer, says the firm's compensations program is grounded in three principles.

First, the company aims to recruit managers and workers who are in the top quartile of the technology market, and therefore pays top-quartile compensation. But, he points out, "the variable portion of compensation gets paid only when the company achieves top-quartile performance relative to its peers."

Second, the firm asks senior executives to purchase the equivalent of 10% of their base pay in Planar shares on the open market. These purchases are in addition to the shares that an executive might acquire through the company's stock option or other equity compensation plan. Planar rewards such purchases by granting nine options with each share bought. "Falling share prices hurt shareholders much more than option holders," Krishnamurthy notes.

Third, the company pays variable employee compensation only after shareholder dividends have been paid, and then pays according to an inverse hierarchy. This means that line workers must be paid their full bonus before any of their superiors. Next in line are middle managers, followed by senior executives, and, lastly, the CEO.

"This approach reflects the direct link between stewardship responsibility and influence," says Krishnamurthy. "The CEO is last in line, and therefore the primary shock absorber, because he has the greatest ability to influence corporate performance."

Incentive Plan Menu

Lincoln National, a Philadelphia-based financial services firm, recently replaced its traditional employee stock options plan with a new LTIP that allows employees to choose from a menu of variable compensation currencies. For each eligible position, the firm determines a specific LTIP value, and the employee designates the currency in which she would like it paid, says George

Davis, the senior vice president of human resources. To compensate for the differences in risk associated with each currency, the company provides stock options at 100% of value, stock at 80%, and cash at 67%.

Another feature of Lincoln's new plan is that the vesting requirements of granted shares and options now include a performance component. The performance

Compensation Complexities

Edward Lawler, professor of management and organization at University of Southern California's Marshall School of Business and the author of *Treat People Right!* (Jossey-Bass/John Wiley & Sons, 2003), is an unabashed advocate of equity compensation at every level of the organization.

Workers below the senior management level who hold equity, he says, may perceive the link between their job performance and the firm's stock price as weak, but they nonetheless retain a certain pride of ownership. Lawler fears that companies will back away from options more for people at these levels than for senior executives; doing so, he says, would set back the practice of broad-based equity compensation.

Some companies have clearly erred in granting options that vest too quickly, Lawler notes. That focuses managers heavily on short-term earnings and share price, ultimately harming the company and undermining credibility. If options are to have a role, he emphasizes, it must be a long-term one.

measures—total shareholder return, ROE, and operating income—must reach the 60th percentile of an industry peer group before the plan rewards employees. However, the rewards are doubled if performance reaches the 75th percentile. "Our new long-term incentive plan is highly leveraged, more shareholder-focused, and has rigorous performance standards," says Jon Boscia, Lincoln's chairman and CEO.

Lincoln's new LTIP covers approximately 60 of the firm's top executives, says Davis. A similar plan that rewards only with performance-restricted stock extends deeper into the organization.

Limited-Choice Plans

Some 80,000 to 90,000 employees in the United States and Canada are eligible to participate in Citigroup's stock options plan, so even minor plan changes can have serious bottom-line consequences.

Still, the company revised the plan in an effort to make it more attractive to employees and easier to control. For example, one major change enables participants in the stock option program to receive a portion of their option grant as restricted stock (one share per four options), says Sheri Meyer-Hanover, Citigroup's director of global equity compensation. Similarly, the firm offers a feature in the restricted stock program allowing employees to reduce their restricted stock by 25% and receive four options for every share of stock. While

Citigroup's equity compensation program isn't necessarily a full cafeteria plan, Meyer-Hanover notes, it does provide more choice to employees.

To exert a greater level of control over stock-based compensation programs, Citigroup reduced the exercise period for employee options from the traditional 10 years to six for all future grants and added a mandatory holding period of two years for all shares purchased from options.

Reprint U0312C

About the Contributors

Charles Wardell is a contributor to *Harvard Management Update*.

Loren Gary is editor of Newsletters at HBS Publishing.

Adam Tobler is a contributor to *Harvard Management Update*.

Anne Field, based in Pelham, N.Y., writes for a number of major business publications.

Theodore Kinni is based in Williamsburg, Virginia. He has authored or ghostwritten seven books.

Jennifer McFarland is a contributor to *Harvard Management Update*.

John Case is a contributor to *Harvard Management Update*.

Lauren Keller Johnson is a contributor to *Harvard Management Update*.

Kristen B. Donahue is a contributor to *Harvard Management Update*.

Frederick F. Reichheld is director emeritus and a fellow of Bain & Company and author of *Loyalty Rules! How Today's Leaders Build Lasting Relationships* (HBS Press, 2001).

Peter Jacobs is a contributor to *Harvard Management Update*.

Harvard Business Review Paperback Series

The Harvard Business Review Paperback Series offers the best thinking on cutting-edge management ideas from the world's leading thinkers, researchers, and managers. Designed for leaders who believe in the power of ideas to change business, these books will be useful to managers at all levels of experience, but especially senior executives and general managers. In addition, this series is widely used in training and executive development programs.

These books are priced at $19.95 U.S.
Price subject to change.

Title	Product #
Harvard Business Review **Interviews with CEOs**	3294
Harvard Business Review on **Advances in Strategy**	8032
Harvard Business Review on **Appraising Employee Performance**	7685
Harvard Business Review on **Becoming a High Performance Manager**	1296
Harvard Business Review on **Brand Management**	1445
Harvard Business Review on **Breakthrough Leadership**	8059
Harvard Business Review on **Breakthrough Thinking**	181X
Harvard Business Review on **Building Personal and Organizational Resilience**	2721
Harvard Business Review on **Business and the Environment**	2336
Harvard Business Review on **The Business Value of IT**	9121
Harvard Business Review on **Change**	8842
Harvard Business Review on **Compensation**	701X
Harvard Business Review on **Corporate Ethics**	273X
Harvard Business Review on **Corporate Governance**	2379
Harvard Business Review on **Corporate Responsibility**	2748
Harvard Business Review on **Corporate Strategy**	1429
Harvard Business Review on **Crisis Management**	2352
Harvard Business Review on **Culture and Change**	8369
Harvard Business Review on **Customer Relationship Management**	6994

Title	Product #
Harvard Business Review on **Decision Making**	5572
Harvard Business Review on **Developing Leaders**	5003
Harvard Business Review on **Doing Business in China**	6387
Harvard Business Review on **Effective Communication**	1437
Harvard Business Review on **Entrepreneurship**	9105
Harvard Business Review on **Finding and Keeping the Best People**	5564
Harvard Business Review on **Innovation**	6145
Harvard Business Review on **The Innovative Enterprise**	130X
Harvard Business Review on **Knowledge Management**	8818
Harvard Business Review on **Leadership**	8834
Harvard Business Review on **Leadership at the Top**	2756
Harvard Business Review on **Leadership in a Changed World**	5011
Harvard Business Review on **Leading in Turbulent Times**	1806
Harvard Business Review on **Managing Diversity**	7001
Harvard Business Review on **Managing High-Tech Industries**	1828
Harvard Business Review on **Managing People**	9075
Harvard Business Review on **Managing Projects**	6395
Harvard Business Review on **Managing the Value Chain**	2344
Harvard Business Review on **Managing Uncertainty**	9083
Harvard Business Review on **Managing Your Career**	1318
Harvard Business Review on **Marketing**	8040
Harvard Business Review on **Measuring Corporate Performance**	8826
Harvard Business Review on **Mergers and Acquisitions**	5556
Harvard Business Review on **The Mind of the Leader**	6409
Harvard Business Review on **Motivating People**	1326
Harvard Business Review on **Negotiation**	2360
Harvard Business Review on **Nonprofits**	9091
Harvard Business Review on **Organizational Learning**	6153
Harvard Business Review on **Strategic Alliances**	1334
Harvard Business Review on **Strategies for Growth**	8850
Harvard Business Review on **Teams That Succeed**	502X
Harvard Business Review on **Turnarounds**	6366
Harvard Business Review on **What Makes a Leader**	6374
Harvard Business Review on **Work and Life Balance**	3286

Management Dilemmas: Case Studies from the Pages of Harvard Business Review

How often do you wish you could turn to a panel of experts to guide you through tough management situations? The Management Dilemmas series provides just that. Drawn from the pages of *Harvard Business Review,* each insightful volume poses several perplexing predicaments and shares the problem-solving wisdom of leading experts. Engagingly written, these solutions-oriented collections help managers make sound judgment calls when addressing every-day management dilemmas.

These books are priced at $19.95 U.S.
Price subject to change.

Title	Product #
Management Dilemmas: **When Change Comes Undone**	5038
Management Dilemmas: **When Good People Behave Badly**	5046
Management Dilemmas: **When Marketing Becomes a Minefield**	5054
Management Dilemmas: **When People Are the Problem**	7138
Management Dilemmas: **When Your Strategy Stalls**	712X

Harvard Business Essentials

In the fast-paced world of business today, everyone needs a personal resource—a place to go for advice, coaching, background information, or answers. The Harvard Business Essentials series fits the bill. Concise and straightforward, these books provide highly practical advice for readers at all levels of experience. Whether you are a new manager interested in expanding your skills or an experienced executive looking to stay on top, these solution-oriented books give you the reliable tips and tools you need to improve your performance and get the job done. Harvard Business Essentials titles will quickly become your constant companions and trusted guides.

These books are priced at $19.95 U.S., except as noted.
Price subject to change.

Title	Product #
Harvard Business Essentials: **Negotiation**	1113
Harvard Business Essentials: **Managing Creativity and Innovation**	1121
Harvard Business Essentials: **Managing Change and Transition**	8741
Harvard Business Essentials: **Hiring and Keeping the Best People**	875X
Harvard Business Essentials: **Finance for Managers**	8768
Harvard Business Essentials: **Business Communication**	113X
Harvard Business Essentials: **Manager's Toolkit ($24.95)**	2896
Harvard Business Essentials: **Managing Projects Large and Small**	3213
Harvard Business Essentials: **Creating Teams with an Edge**	290X
Harvard Business Essentials: **Entrepreneur's Toolkit**	4368
Harvard Business Essentials: **Coaching and Mentoring**	435X
Harvard Business Essentials: **Crisis Management**	4376

The Results-Driven Manager

The Results-Driven Manager series collects timely articles from *Harvard Management Update* and *Harvard Management Communication Letter* to help senior to middle managers sharpen their skills, increase their effectiveness, and gain a competitive edge. Presented in a concise, accessible format to save managers valuable time, these books offer authoritative insights and techniques for improving job performance and achieving immediate results.

These books are priced at $14.95 U.S.
Price subject to change.

Title	Product #
The Results-Driven Manager: **Face-to-Face Communications for Clarity and Impact**	3477
The Results-Driven Manager: **Managing Yourself for the Career You Want**	3469
The Results-Driven Manager: **Presentations That Persuade and Motivate**	3493
The Results-Driven Manager: **Teams That Click**	3507
The Results-Driven Manager: **Winning Negotiations That Preserve Relationships**	3485
The Results-Driven Manager: **Dealing with Difficult People**	6344
The Results-Driven Manager: **Taking Control of Your Time**	6352
The Results-Driven Manager: **Getting People on Board**	6360
The Results-Driven Manager: **Motivating People for Improved Performance**	7790
The Results-Driven Manager: **Becoming an Effective Leader**	7804
The Results-Driven Manager: **Managing Change to Reduce Resistance**	7812

How to Order

Harvard Business School Press publications are available worldwide
from your local bookseller or online retailer.
You can also call

1-800-668-6780

Our product consultants are available to help you
8:00 a.m.–6:00 p.m., Monday–Friday, Eastern Time.
Outside the U.S. and Canada, call: 617-783-7450
Please call about special discounts for quantities greater than ten.

You can order online at

www.HBSPress.org